Formal Education
and
Culture Change

Formal
Education and Culture

Change

A MODERN
APACHE INDIAN
COMMUNITY
AND
GOVERNMENT
EDUCATION
PROGRAMS

Edward A. Parmee

THE UNIVERSITY OF ARIZONA PRESS
Tucson, Arizona

THE UNIVERSITY OF ARIZONA PRESS

This book is dedicated to every man, woman and youth who would seek to make this world a better place for all mankind to live in; and to Ed Morrow, an educator with heart, who died trying.

A Statement by the Author

EACH PERSON WHO READS THIS BOOK will undoubtedly see it in a different light. There will be those who agree and those who disagree. Some will find it useful and others will wish they had saved their pennies. A few may seek to emulate the efforts described here, while a certain few, I am sure, will display aspects of this work as examples of how not to conduct a study. But none of these concerns me as much as the reader who attempts to make me say what I have not intended.

I readily admit that much of what is included in this monograph is critical of numerous aspects of the Bureau of Indian Affairs and state public education programs on the San Carlos Reservation. It would be wrong, however, to interpret such a critique as a wholesale condemnation of these programs or of the agencies and personnel that administer them. The person to whom this book is dedicated is an outstanding example of some of the praiseworthy aspects of these programs, and there were other equally dedicated people at work. But in order to evoke change one must emphasize the inadequacies of the status quo, and evoking a change for the better—in attitude, policy, and procedure—is without question a primary interest of this author.

As I am critical of the attitudes and behavior of some non-Apaches at the time of this study, I am also critical of those Apaches who could have contributed more to the development of their reservation community, but for selfish, personal reasons did not. Such individuals found it far easier to curse all "outsiders," rather than to seek out those who were sincerely dedicated and work with them in an effort to create

vii

a greater mutual understanding. On the more positive side, I have the greatest admiration for those Apache citizens who, in spite of intense pressures from many sides, risked their own personal comforts and security to work long days and nights for the sake of their fellow Apaches, to prove the real strength of the people's pride and resourcefulness in solving their own problems.

This book is written in vigorous opposition to the policy or program that seeks to vivisect the population of a community into its live, successive generations without concern for the family, neighborhood, or the surviving native unit of traditional social organization (i.e. the Apache *gotah*), as vital, durable, interdependent and potentially productive social and economic units in which all existing age groups interact for mutual benefit and security. Ignorance of the dynamics of these social units or disregard for their importance within the community during periods of stress and widespread change can lead to much conflict and social disharmony, creating chaos instead of constructive change.

Hence, this book has not been written to provide the reader with a current and definitive description of the San Carlos Apaches and their reservation, but rather as a demonstration of what can happen to a community—any community—when it is manipulated by outside sources and its people are neither trained nor given an increasing share of the responsibility for their own affairs, when they are deprived of their traditional heritage while pressured to accept change, and when their social, political, and economic institutions are disrupted without provision for immediate or adequate replacement.

Finally, it is hoped that from reading this study there will be those who, like me, can see many ways in which the experiences of the San Carlos Apaches can constructively serve people with similar problems in other communities of the world, provided that the necessary modifications are made to meet differing local conditions.

As the number and size of social and economic development programs increase each day, the need for better mutual understanding between the *objects* of change (i.e., the people of a community) and the *instigators of change* (i.e., agency personnel) also increases. If, as educators, we would claim to be a somewhat enlightened form of instigator, then we must show a greater awareness of the values, orientations, needs, aspirations, and traditional pride of the people with whom we intend to work. To achieve this in itself requires a great effort, both physical and emotional, but it provides the only secure foundation for a successful development program. Similarly, making the people aware of our goals and orientations and of the potential administrative complexities and cultural repercussions involved in undertaking such a program may better prepare them for some of the problems that will inevitably arise out of the process of change once it has been initiated.

Such are the responsibilities of the educator. To instigate is not enough, for change is a continual process that must be constantly guided if the most beneficial effects are to be realized. If a nation or a person undertakes to initiate change among a people who are unprepared to meet the consequences, then it becomes a moral obligation to work with the people and teach them how to cope with the challenges that lie ahead. Under such circumstances, then, it goes without saying that education, when established for the purpose of initiating culture change, is not for those who are but casually interested or faint of heart.

●　　　●　　　●

It is difficult within the limitations of these acknowledgements to enumerate the contributions of so many which have now, finally, come to fruition in this book. To those mentioned here, and to the many unnamed who unselfishly gave of their time and knowledge, I wish to express my sincere gratitude.

My thanks to the National Science Foundation and the Comins Fund for their support of the San Carlos Project, which made possible the research substantiating this report; to Dr. Edward H. Spicer, my research director, whose patience, persistent encouragement, and careful guidance gave meaning to so much of my work and professional inspiration to so many of my untempered thoughts; to Marshall Townsend, University of Arizona Press Director, for his expert criticisms and suggestions; and to all of the faculty and staff in the Department of Anthropology, who, over the past years, have never once failed to offer me their generous aid and support.

My most heartfelt appreciation also goes out to the people of the San Carlos Reservation community and those educators and officials from the Phoenix area and school systems adjacent to the reservation who showed me great hospitality, sincere friendship, and abundant cooperation in spite of the many times they were inconvenienced by "that skinny White guy from the University":

San Carlos Apache Tribal members: Marvin Mull, Tom Nosie, Oliver Talgo, Jess Stevens, Clarence Wesley, members of the tribal council; Floyd Mull, Joe Bullis, David Sine, Cecelia Sneezy, Elson Brown, members of the tribal health and education committees; and the many Apache students interviewed.

Educators: Ed Morrow, Phil Premy, Eldon Randall, Max Oliger, Chuck Bernardoni, Paul Bramlet, Sam Mackey, Mr. Miller, Mr. Lemminger, and numerous hard-working school teachers.

BIA and USPHS Officials: Mary Ethel Stickney, Clinton Rivers, Al Garcia, Dr. Urich, Britton Goodie, Ruth M. Bronson, Charles Rives, Al Purchase, and Lena Nelson.

Other members of the San Carlos Reservation Community: Mr. and Mrs. Joseph Haught, Mr. and Mrs. Camilo Casteneda, Mr. and Mrs. Charles McEvers, Mr. and Mrs. David Perkins, Steve Talbot, Father Bartholemew, Pastors Alfred Uplegger and H. E. Rosine, Reverend Bunny, and the Osbornes.

Finally, my especial thanks to Mrs. Sherry Cutter Belvado, project secretary, for her excellent work in gathering school records and compiling voluminous data files; to Mr. Charles Mull, Sr., my close friend, guide, interpreter, and industrious co-worker, for his profoundly wise insight into many current reservation problems and past developments and for his ever-timely advice, criticism, and reliable assistance throughout the entire duration of the project; and to my dear wife, Leila, for her patience, understanding, and unfailing support throughout the writing of this monograph.

E. A. P.

Contents

Charts and Tables

CHART

TABLES

The Setting and the Project

IT IS THE INTENTION of the author to show, by means of a small community study within the society of a minority American culture, how education, when used to impose culture change at a rate and of a nature that is defined solely by the convenience and ethnocentric policies of the dominant culture, can create serious social and psychological conflicts within the minority society. These conflicts can actually inhibit the very adjustment or change that the dominant culture is trying to promote. Furthermore, they can affect the potential human resources of the minority society in such a deleterious manner that the people are left morally weakened, culturally deprived, and economically dependent.

The subject of this study will be the San Carlos Apache Indians of the Southwestern United States.

For centuries empires have risen out of the rubble of conflict to dominate some portion of mankind, only to disintegrate, eventually leaving a distinct and indelible mark in the pattern of man's cultural heritage. The bases of these empires have been complex, as were the causes of their eventual decline, involving social and economic, political, and religious factors. Throughout the course of recorded history in the Western Hemisphere, however, the major factors influencing the colonial policies of conquering empires have had social and religious elements, based on concepts of Christian ethics and the evangelical obligations of "civilized nations."

Formalized, systematic education under the strict control of the dominant culture has, since the days of Spanish conquest, been the primary tool for the implementation of culture

1

change among the native peoples of the Americas. Molded in the forge of Christianized Europe and tempered by its own growing technological needs, formal education held for Western man the key to civilized greatness, through its training in reason, discipline, ethics, and knowledge for all men. So firmly imbedded was this belief in the positive evolutionary force of education that much of Western man's colonial effort was guided by the zeal of his evangelical desires. Within the last one hundred years a rather striking example of this phenomenon, where formal education has been used as an applied process for induced culture change, is the treatment by the dominant U.S. society of the reservation American Indians.

The Land and Its People

To the tourist, speedily making his way through the rugged, arid low-country along Arizona's Highway 70, the San Carlos Apache Reservation must leave an impression very much like that of an iceberg on the unsuspecting sea-traveler. It takes less than an hour to drive from the east boundary to the west, and if he does not pause a while at Bylas, the small Apache community split by a brief segment of the road, the traveler might never realize that this is the "Land of the San Carlos Apaches," a place of many contrasts and much contradiction.

The San Carlos Reservation sprawls across three counties of east central Arizona, encompassing a total of more than 1.6 million acres or 2,600 square miles, yet it is inhabited by fewer than 5,000 Apaches. (In comparison, the state of Delaware includes only 2,057 square miles, and holds about 500,000 people.) Although much of the terrain is rough and mountainous, there are large, flat mesas and rolling range lands in the south and western portions and the higher elevations. While lower areas of the reservation are quite arid, receiving only 12 inches of precipitation a year, in the higher areas the rainfall can frequently be twice this amount, permitting streams to flow the year 'round.

The dry, semi-desert regions support little more than sparse grasses, cacti, and scrub growth except along the San

Carlos and Gila rivers, which flow beneath the surface throughout much of the year to feed the man-made San Carlos Lake. In the northern mountains and high plateau areas, however, rich grasslands and broad forests of ponderosa pine create a vast refuge for deer, mountain lion, and wild turkey.

About 75% of the resident Apache population inhabit the adjacent communities of San Carlos and Peridot on the western end of the reservation. The remainder live about 20 miles distant at Bylas. In addition, some 500 tribal members live and work off the reservation. In apparent contradiction of the "vanishing race" theory, more than half of the population is under the age of 21, with every evidence of an imminent increase in numbers as time goes on. Also, better than 95% of the Apaches here are classified as "full-bloods" according to a Bureau of Indian Affairs survey (The San Carlos Apache Tribal Council 1962:4).

The primary economic activity of the San Carlos Apaches today is the production of cattle. Five livestock corporations composed of tribal members manage some 12,000 head of cattle, producing a gross annual income of close to one million dollars. While this may seem like a sizeable source of income, only one-third of the Apache families own cattle, and of that number some 69% receive less than $1,000 per year from the sale of livestock. Federal government and tribal payrolls provide consistent wages for some Apaches, while to a more limited extent, welfare, farming, mining, forestry, and part-time wage work also contribute to the local economy. According to the 1962 economic development survey of the tribal council:

> For the average Indian family, making a living is a combination of part time wage work, credit against cattle income, with the slack filled in by welfare payments, surplus commodities and unemployment compensation (The San Carlos Apache Tribal Council 1962:5).

Chronic unemployment and underemployment have sapped the strength of the reservation economy for many years. Discouraged by the lack of reservation employment opportunities, yet often unwilling and unprepared to leave the reservation for whatever work they might find, many San Carlos Apaches today have succumbed to the paternal care of federal, state, and local agencies operating on the reservation to provide individuals and families with at least minimum subsistence. The solution of this dismal predicament is the primary goal and most strenuous activity of Apache tribal leaders today. As tribal chairman Marvin Mull once explained:

> When we are talking about changing values . . . we are talking about trying to better ourselves on the reservation. Let me show you what I mean by telling you some of the things that we are trying to do at San Carlos. First, with our tribal enterprises, we still have White employees in some of our key positions. We want to gradually replace these White people by our own Indian boys. To do this, we have to have these boys qualified, we have to have them educated. The thinking among some of the Indians on the reservation, especially among the older people, is that when an Indian finishes High School, twelfth grade, then he's ready for a big job, but that isn't so. The requirements for some of the key positions that we have on the reservation require much higher than High School education (Mull 1963:31).

The Problem and the Research

As the San Carlos Apaches emerged into the second half of the twentieth century, it was clearly evident to all concerned that the lack of adequate educational standards throughout the local population was still a major stumbling block to improving reservation conditions. The average level of education for tribal members was estimated to be at the eighth grade, far too low for most skilled jobs (The San Carlos Apache Tribal Council 1962:20). Indian Bureau and public school officials were concerned about the high rate of school drop-outs and daily absenteeism, as well as the extremely low percentage of high school and college graduates. Tribal leaders, meanwhile, complained that their students were receiving inferior training and discriminatory treatment from both public and federal school programs.

In response to a request from both tribal and BIA offices, the University of Arizona through the sponsorship of the National Science Foundation began a two and one-half year research project on the San Carlos Reservation. The chairman of the project was Dr. Edward H. Spicer of the Department of Anthropology. His assistant and primary field researcher is the author of this book.

The data for the ensuing study came from files of the San Carlos School Project, and include official school and court records, case histories, interviews, and field notes recording a variety of subjects and incidents reflecting the operations of the entire school program, the attitudes of children, parents, and non-Indians, and many facets of reservation life.

The major portion of the data for this study was gathered by the author while residing at San Carlos, Arizona from February, 1959 until July, 1961. Throughout the course of this period he lived in a camping trailer parked in an area known as the "Farm Station," where a number of Indian and non-Indian tribal employees had their homes.

In an effort to become acquainted with reservation life and the many key people and institutions that participated in it, the author was encouraged to make use of every opportunity to work with Apaches while learning from them. Since pure research meant little to the average reservation inhabitant, who had vital daily problems to solve and very practical tasks to fulfill, it was important that the field worker of this study become well integrated into the active agencies responsible for performing local daily services for the Apache people.

Thus, in the summer of 1959, he became a camp supervisor for Apache teen-age boys who were working in the mountains earning money for personal school expenses. Throughout the 1959-60 school year, with the aid of a male informant paid from project funds, the author acted as an unofficial truant officer and guidance counselor, sharing the daily rounds with a native tribal employee. During this time the project maintained an office with a full-time Apache secretary in the old San Carlos School building, as a base of operations.

Assigned from the very beginning by the tribal council to work in cooperation with the tribal education committee, the author acted for more than a year as its secretary and treasurer, working with the members in weekly projects, such as the local Apache newspaper, and traveling annually with some of its leaders to distant schools and education conferences. During the last year of the study the author worked as a member of the tribal health committee. He also cooperated with local interested citizens to open a community library that received many of its materials from the State of Arizona Library Extension System.

Throughout all of these activities affiliations were maintained with the local school, health, welfare, and law enforcement agencies. The author had particularly close contact with such personalities as the vice-chairman of the tribal council and head of the health and education committees, the local tribal juvenile officers, the BIA reservation principal, the BIA social worker, the six local school principals and many of their teaching staff, the tribal judges, the local American Friends Service Committee representative, and numerous Indian and non-Indian inhabitants of the reservation community, many of whom were close personal friends.

Investigation of the records made during the first year of the study revealed that serious academic and social problems existed for many Apache teen-agers. The rate of academic progress for Apaches beyond the fourth grade level was significantly below that for non-Indians. Boarding school and juvenile court records indicated severe social and emotional problems for a large segment of the Apache teen-age population. There was in addition an exceptionally poor response to opportunities for higher education and career employment among the Apache youth, as reflected in drop-out and employment records, and post high school academic enrollment.

A continued analysis in depth throughout the study revealed a great many interesting factors contributing to the poor conditions for effective formal education on the San Carlos Reservation.

The primary problems of teen-age Apache students, as indicated by the available school and juvenile records, grew out of the many conflicts between the school systems and the various social, cultural, and economic forces existing on the San Carlos Reservation, producing an environment so unstable that it actually inhibited the learning process of the teen-age Apache child as he participated in the formal program of education to which he was committed. It is believed that these conflicts came from three basic areas of existing conditions on the reservation.

First, there was an apparent lack of favorable community influences to help the Apache student in his search for higher levels of education and socio-economic conditions. Reservation unemployment stood at an average far above the rest of the nation (Arizona Commission of Indian Affairs 1964b). There were few Apache models of success for the younger generation to follow. Many tribal leaders were poorly educated in spite of their high political status. Numerous social pressures, remnants of traditional Apache customs and beliefs, were imposed from time to time on Apaches seeking to assimilate non-Indian habits. These occurred in the form of public hostility, avoidance, or even political and economic discrimination, if the individual was in a position where he needed tribal support.

Secondly, it was learned that in the case of many Apache families, there was both inadequate and inconsistent adult support of the Apache students and the overall program of education to which they were committed. Much of this "apathy," which at times even turned into passive or open resistance, resulted from a variety of factors:

a) Widespread family poverty and unemployment had discouraged many adults and had turned their attention to the immediate relief of pressing economic problems.

b) The continual breakdown of Apache family solidarity and authority had blocked many of the normal channels of family support.

c) Many of the Apache adults were ignorant of the real aims and methods of the education program, and hence hesitated to give it their full support. Those who possibly misunderstood or disagreed with certain aspects of the education program offered resistance to it because they felt that it conflicted with some of their traditional Apache values.

d) Many Apache adults showed resentment towards the program of education for their children because they had been for so long kept out of the policy-making and operational aspects of the program.

Finally, there were many problems within the framework of the education program itself that had created conflicts for the Apache students. It was found that there were many inconsistencies between the policies and methods used by the three major school systems employed: federal, public, and mission schools. Investigation of the academic work at the primary levels on the reservation showed that many Apache students entering high school were poorly prepared to meet the existing requirements.

A review of the guidance and counseling services available to Apache teen-agers revealed a wide-spread inability on the part of the various school systems to evaluate the problems and potentials of these students properly. The orientation of the entire program, in fact, was towards the assimilation of Apaches into the Anglo culture, an aim which was diametrically opposed to the desires of most Apaches, while the efforts to bring the goals and operation of the program into more extended agreement with the needs and desires of the Apache people were either weak or non-existent.

A study of this nature has its value in the fact that some of its interpretations will have broad as well as specialized application. Educators and tribal leaders throughout the country, for example, do not understand why the vast sums of money spent thus far on the education of Indian youngsters have not produced more college graduates and skilled workers. This study will attempt to show why so many Apache students have a sense of failure almost built into their personalities, a condition which has more and more serious consequences as the youngsters approach higher levels of formal education.

Many of the current techniques used in federal and public schools for evaluating the problems and potentials of American Indian students are open to serious question regarding their validity and effectiveness. This study will try to illustrate and evaluate this problem in the light of observations made from the program of education for San Carlos Apaches.

There are many sources in the literature today describing the nature and intensity of teen-age problems among the youth of lower socio-economic minority groups in the United States. Since many of the problems described in this study will be similar to those found in the literature, this additional knowledge should increase our understanding of the problem as a whole.

CHAPTER 1

Formal Education: A Technique For Inducing Culture Change

IN ORDER TO ACHIEVE A BETTER UNDERSTANDING of the data to be presented regarding the program of education for the San Carlos Apaches, let us first examine rather briefly the growth and refinement of formal education as it has come to be applied as a technique for inducing culture change.

From the Ancients to British India

In ancient Greece, education was decidedly the privilege of the wealthy. According to Protagoras: "Those who can best afford to give this education give most of it. Their sons go earliest to school and leave it latest" (Boyd 1952: 19).

During much of the period of the Roman Empire, formal education was both furthered by the personal interests of some of her emperors—i.e., Hadrian (117-138 A.D.) and Marcus Aurelius (161-180 A.D.)—and disrupted by periods of civil strife and political chaos (Boyd 1952: 80). As Christianity progressed throughout the Empire, however, a "new moral and intellectual force was being set free" which had a much more lasting effect on the growth of formal education (Boyd 1952: 82).

Although much of the formal schooling in those times was considered by upper-class Christians to be "paganistic," because of the dominance of Greek influences, church leaders like Tertullian (circa 160 A.D.) begrudgingly admitted the need for education among Christian youth: "How otherwise could anyone acquire human wisdom, or learn to direct his thoughts and actions?" (Boyd 1952: 83).

Saint Augustine, in the sixth century A.D., emphasized the need for learning among Christians from a standpoint that gave formal education a powerful and far reaching impetus: the need to educate Christian missionaries in order to propagate the teachings of the Church (Boyd 1952: 91). Since much of the missionary work was being done by illiterate laymen who volunteered their services and their lives to the Church, the leaders of the Church took hold of this challenge and soon developed a system of schools (such as the "bishops' schools" in England) that withstood many of the ravages of the Dark Ages.

During the sixteenth century, as Spain developed her colonies in the New World, the responsibility for "civilizing" the native inhabitants—that is to say, of educating and converting them to the Catholic religion and the Spanish way of life— was left to the care of the clergy, who took up the challenge with zeal (Sanchez 1944: 30-32). Cortes himself saw to it that men like Pedro de Gante, lay brother of the Order of St. Francis, were encouraged to come to New Spain to build schools, construct churches, and eventually to develop a system of education that would transform the "hopeless task of cultivating aboriginal minds" into an aggressive and effective campaign for the "transmission of European culture" (Jacobsen 1938: 39-43).

Three hundred years later, in an opposing sector of the world, the East India Company fell heir to the missionary zeal of such men as Charles Grant, William Wilberforce, Edward Thornton, and Zachary Macaulay, when in 1813 they convinced Parliament that the introduction of Western education into India was an "obligation derived from the duty of Great Britain 'to promote the interests and happiness of the native inhabitants' " (McCully 1940: 17-18). Along with this declaration of principle, the new East India Act provided statutory sanction for annual educational appropriations, and the doors to Christian missionary enterprises were opened wide (McCully 1940: 17-18).

The underlying philosophy of these acts was expressed in two primary objectives:

1) the establishment of a new kind of "moral order" in India, replacing the Hindu "superstitions" that op-

posed the acceptance of Christianity and its prescribed code of ethics; and

2) the introduction of Western European culture into India, in the form of the arts, philosophy, and science, through the medium of English instruction (McCully 1940: 12; Keay 1959: 202).

"These acquisitions," Charles Grant predicted, "would silently undermine, and at length subvert, the fabric of errors . . ." (i.e., lack of scientific knowledge, adherence to traditional customs and religions, etc.) to ultimately raise the "decadent society" of Hindu India to the level of European civilization (McCully 1940: 12). The inception of the British system of formal education did much to "Westernize" the upcoming generations of Indian society; barely one hundred years later India was in a position to declare herself a unified nation of English speaking peoples, with enough of a "Westernized" social, political, and economic system to compete as an independent republic with the other "Westernized" countries of the world (Keay 1959: 202).

Among the American Indians of the United States, however, history has woven a different plot, with patterns of far greater complexity, and as yet no indication of a triumphant finale. Here, too, formal education was eventually developed as the ultimate weapon against what was regarded as barbarism, the steel-edged blade to carve the "savage mentality" into a likeness of "Civilized Man." But that is where the similarity between the history of the Indians in India and those of the United States stops, and this is where we shall begin to show the differences.

The "Civilization" of America's Indians

Apparently there were no Grants or Macaulays with a strong voice in Parliament when the British began expanding their colonies in the Western Hemisphere. The government had no interest in converting the Indians to Christianity or "civilization," and dealt with them only to acquire land either by purchase or conquest. At best the various tribal groups were treated as "foreign nations" without political or economic status within the framework of the Colonies. As a result, the numerous Indian groups in their communities did not experience the same social, economic, and political development as the Europeans in their ever-expanding settlements. Without citizenship, land rights, or the wherewithal to defend themselves, the Indians remained aliens to be pushed, pitied or parleyed with by the growing tide of empire builders, who moved deeper and deeper into Indian-held territory (Spicer 1962: 344).

After 1776, the new government of the United States continued this policy, pushing the Indians farther and farther westward before the on-rushing tide of settlers. It was only after the management of Indian Affairs was transferred from the War Department to the Department of the Interior that views of a different sort began to take effect.

Out of the era of the Civil War grew burning issues of national recognition about the dignity of all races and the rights of freedom for all men. The conscience of many Anglo-Americans—and more significantly, of their Congress—could no longer bear the guilt of Indian annihilation. Men of influence like Vincent Colyer and General O. O. Howard, representing the federal government, sought to make peace with the Indians, to place them on assigned reservations, and to protect them from Anglo encroachment.

With the establishment of Indian reservations, very rarely located in the most productive areas of the country, many tribal groups were deprived of their traditional economic pursuits. Initially, the government was pleased to offer complete material support to the Indians in return for peaceful coexistence. Soon, however, it became obvious that if these people were ever to become self-supporting, steps would have to be taken to train them to make use of their new and restricted environment. The federal government, through its Department of the Interior, was given the full responsibility for this "program for civilization" (Spicer 1962: 346-347).

The Dawes Act of 1887 crystallized much of this policy, and along with its land allotment program it provided for the establishment of a number of off-reservation boarding schools for the children. Another key feature of this plan was to turn over much of the responsibility for Indian Affairs to the various Christian religious denominations, who were eager to win new converts from the ranks of the "noble red man." As new boarding schools were established under church auspices with missionary teachers and federal subsidy, more and more Indian children were forcibly exposed to the ways of Western man (Spicer 1962: 347-349).

By the turn of the century, the Indian Bureau had relinquished most of its contracts with the various missionary groups and had undertaken the operation of the boarding school program itself. More and more schools were being built on or near the reservations, and by 1917 nearly 7,000 Indian students were enrolled throughout Arizona, New Mexico, Nevada, and Utah (Spicer 1962: 438). As a result of this program of "captive education" many Indian families developed hostile attitudes towards the Indian Bureau, for they sorely resented the disruption of traditional family life. Finally, in 1934, provisions were made for the support of local day school facilities for reservation Indian children.

The Indian Reorganization Act of 1934 made some far-reaching changes in the policies of the Indian Bureau. Instead of encouraging the allotment—and ultimate loss—of reservation lands, allotments were stopped and land was purchased to be added to many of the existing reservations. The suppression of traditional religious activities through restrictive laws and economic support of Christian missionary schools was halted. Federal schools began teaching Indian students to appreciate "favorable" aspects of their traditional cultures, and many boarding schools were either closed or converted into day schools, with provisions made to allow for federal support of the cost of educating Indian children in nearby integrated public schools (Spicer 1962: 351-352).

> The basic idea of the IRA policy was that the cultural assimilation of Indians, individual by individual, as conceived in the former policy of land allotment and boarding school education, disorganized both Indian personality

and communities, and that influences from Anglo culture could best be assimilated through the medium of the tribe as an organized entity set up to deal as a unit with the outside influences (Spicer 1962: 352).

Developments in Indian Education Since the 1950's

Although much of the policy included in the 1934 Indian Reorganization Act is followed to this day, there have been some new developments within the educational phase of the Indian Bureau program. While the expressed philosophy directing the program still aims towards the improvement of Indian communities (Peterson 1948: 9-10), much has been done within the last few years to increase the degree of contact between Indians and Anglos. Chief among these efforts is the establishment of a great many more integrated public schools, substantially supported by federal Johnson-O'Malley funds (Arizona Commission of Indian Affairs 1961-62: 14-18). Some of these new schools are now appearing within the boundaries of the reservations, with federal, state, and local agencies cooperating in their administration.

Since employment opportunities were severely limited on many reservations, the Indian Bureau developed an extensive relocation program for Indian families willing to train and work in metropolitan areas often distant from their native homelands. Thus, by taking advantage of compelling economic needs, the Indian Bureau hoped that many Indian families would be forced into extended contact with Anglos, by living and working in off-reservation non-Indian communities, the eventual result being ultimate assimilation.

Within the last ten years, higher education—that is, academic and vocational training for Indians beyond the high school level—has drawn increasing attention from Indians and non-Indians alike. Vast sums from a wide variety of sources have been invested in scholarships for an ever-increasing number of high school Indian graduates whose records show promise for further training. These students, representatives of their generation, are supposed to go out into the White man's world to learn its ways and then return to their people, leading them into closer alignment with the modern world.

Thus, in slightly more than four bewildered generations, the American Indian has been transformed from a "vanishing race" into a prominent American minority. The White man, too, has experienced a transformation of sorts, and has traded in his repeating rifle for the textbook. The relentless, horse-mounted soldiers in blue have long-since retired, relieved by an army of educators.

Surrounded by a society bewitched by the lure of "progress," the American Indian today has come to learn that "tradition is the enemy of progress" (McCombe, Vogt, & Kluckholn 1951: 82). Amid the cries of a few who extol the value of preserving many Indian traditional beliefs and customs, are heard the firm, unfaltering views of high-ranking educators and Indian Bureau personnel, who maintain that "It becomes apparent that co-mingling or mixture in the melting pot of American education is necessary or basic to the future of the Indian people" (Head 1960: 24).

A large segment of the Indian population today is not willing to have its identity thrown into the "melting-pot" so that it can be absorbed by the dominant Anglo culture. The members of this segment may seek a material standard of living equal to that of the White man, but they do not desire his code of values, nor do they wish to assimilate his cultural heritage: the philosophies, the legends, and the spiritual traditions that identify the Anglo-Americans as a part of "Western Civilization."

> As an Indian tribe, we need to better our standards of living, that's all we're looking for, through education. You cannot change our color, nobody's going to change our color. You can scrub it a hundred times a day and we'll still have our dark skin. All we're asking for is a better way of life and that comes only through education. I hope our youngsters will keep some of these values of their culture, of their religion, of their beliefs, the story of how they have been created. There's a beautiful story about how the Navajos were created. But the histories that are written today are not being written by Navajos;

do you know where they said the Navajos came from? They say they came through Alaska down this way to where we are now. That is not our story; I believe our story. I don't think I came from China. We have a different belief altogether, different legends that we tell to our youngsters, and I believe they should be kept (Wauneka 1963:36).

And this is where much of the conflict lies. While Indians are looking to formal education as a solution to many of their present problems—poverty, poor health, social disintegration, and political impotence, the factors which threaten to destroy the "Indian way of life"—Anglos view formal education as the key process for the peaceful assimilation of all Indian groups. The result is a conflict harboured within the fundamental aims of the program of Indian education itself. It is a conflict that endangers the successful fulfillment of the hopes of either side, and it seriously threatens the great reservoir of human potential inherent in the present and future generations of Indian youth.

CHAPTER 2

Indian Education in the 1960's

ALTHOUGH there are several historical works written about the Apaches of the San Carlos Reservation by such authors as Goodwin (1942), Clum (1928-1931), Spicer (1962) and Kaut (1957), to name a few, there is very little to be found describing the Apaches of the post World War II period. Even less has been written about their specific problems in education, although an occasional conference report was made during the course of this study: Oliger (1961), Parmee (1961), Talbot (1962).

There are, however, quite a few recent studies regarding the personal-social problems of Indian students from other reservations, as well as a number of comprehensive reports discussing Indian education in general. It is from these more recent sources in the literature that a selected number of relevant studies will be reviewed in an attempt to assist the reader in achieving an understanding of the problems and their causes discussed in Chapters 3 and 4.

It will be seen that many of the problems enumerated in the literature are shared by the Apache students, for it has been found that the difference in the problems of students from different tribes is very often one of degree rather than nature. This is borne out by the fact that many research projects in Indian education lump all Indian students together when analyzing the data, just as they frequently lump the findings from all non-Indian students together: e.g., Zintz (1960), Peterson (1948), McGrath et al. (1962). At a 1960 workshop on the problems of Indian students in federal boarding schools, attended by Bureau of Indian Affairs and U.S. Public Health personnel, it was concluded that while there are some unique tribal differences among the Indian children, there are also many basic similarities between the students of different tribes and between their personal and educational problems (Phoenix Indian School 1960).

Perhaps it is even more significant that in the literature one finds historical, social, and economic factors contributing to the personal and educational problems of reservation Indian teen-agers everywhere, which are similar to some of the underlying causes of teen-age problems among the San Carlos Apaches. By comparing the results of previous studies with the observations at San Carlos, it was possible to pinpoint certain fundamental areas of social conflict, economic deprivation, and cultural instability.

There are many examples cited in the literature of unfavorable community conditions existing on American Indian reservations. In the area of employment, for example, a resources development study on the San Carlos Apache Reservation by the Stanford Research Institute in 1954, showed that: "At the present time, the reservation's 1,623,000 acres furnish employment for approximately three-fourths of the nearly 1,000 family heads who are resident members of the tribe" (Robison et al. 1954:9).

In 1964, however, the Arizona Commission of Indian Affairs published figures even less favorable—though possibly not as well substantiated—than the Stanford Research Institute study. According to the ACIA, 500 (approximate figure only) out of a total male labor force of 750 were unemployed. For the women, 100 (approximate figure only) out of 130 claimed to be unemployed. The report states that no more than 80 Apaches were employed on the reservation (Arizona Commission of Indian Affairs 1946b).*

Conditions among the Sioux of North and South Dakota have from time to time been compared with those of the San Carlos Apache. A look at some employment figures cited in

---

*The author is assuming that these figures refer to full-time employees only. Temporary employment increases suddenly during the brief round-up and cattle-sale period.

the recently completed Oglala Sioux Educational Project by Murray and Rosalie Wax shows that in 1956, out of 2,606 Sioux families, 58.6% claimed an annual income of under $1,000. Such a sum seems less surprising when one is aware of the fact that in that same year over 52.9% of the heads of Sioux families were unemployed. The South Dakota unemployment figure for 1950 was 2.7%. State the authors of this report: ". . . Originally, the 'Indian problem' was regarded as one of cultural assimilation, whereas today the concern is the economic misery and social inferiority of the Indian" (Wax et al. 1964: 23-24).

Economic and occupational conditions on the San Carlos Apache Reservation have become so acute that a special appeal to the U.S. Congress was made by the tribe in 1963, to establish one of the first National Service Corps programs on their reservation.

There is a critical need for programs on the San Carlos Reservation to improve economic conditions and to deal with the problems of social and cultural adjustment. A large portion of the potential labor force is either unemployed or underemployed. According to figures prepared by the Bureau of Indian Affairs, the labor force on the San Carlos Reservation is 1,500 persons, of whom 75 percent or 1,225, are unemployed. Living conditions on the reservation are equally deplorable with almost all of the families living in one or two-room shacks, without electricity, plumbing, a nearby water source, adequate light, heat or ventilation (*Apache Drumbeat*, July, 1963:1)

Under such extreme conditions of poverty and unemployment, home life and schooling are bound to suffer. As people live from day to day in "economic misery" the simple tasks of home life, such as getting the children off to school each day, become great hurdles, and any plans for the future become swallowed up by the overriding problems of today. In such circumstances parental support of the school program is often overwhelmed by the size and complexity of the daily family trials. Some Anglos call this "apathy," but in an average Anglo middle-class family the task of complying with local school requirements is far less difficult. Green, in a report to the Co-ordinating Council for Research in Indian Education, describes very candidly the daily chores of many a reservation Indian household:

Let's take a close look at Elsie and her family. Elsie is a seventeen year old Navajo girl, a high school junior, who lives in a mud and log hogan with elderly parents and five younger brothers and sisters. She is superintending the younger children in getting the clothes ready for the following school week and seeing to it that everyone gets a bath and washes their hair because as Elsie puts it, she wants "all the kids to go to school looking nice."

Now if that sounds like a reasonably simply expectation, let me describe just what is entailed in achieving these results. Water is always hard to come by, even though in recent years many new windmills have been erected for the people's use. Sometimes the roads to the windmills are impassable, or the water at the windmill may be frozen. This was the case during last winter's visit on the Reservation, so Elsie, as did the other families, melted snow most of the winter, using the water for all purposes including drinking, cooking, and laundering. Now it is surprising and infinitely disappointing to see how little water results from melting a heaping bucket of snow. Repeated trips must be made out into the cold, often through slush and mud, to find clean snow in order to keep the water supply replenished. This task kept Elsie and the children going in and out of the hogan constantly. When it is extremely cold, this poses a heating problem. When the snows thaw, great quantities of mud are tracked in causing further difficulties in housekeeping. Though Elsie constantly wields a broom it is a discouraging job at best. At all times Elsie keeps buckets of snow on top of the oil dum stove, which is located in the center of the hogan. She is never able to keep enough water melted and heated at one time to fill a tub, so she and the children use basins and wash the clothes by hand. If weather permits, these are hung out of doors. If it is snowing, or if the clothes are apt to freeze a few pieces at a time are hung on a short line in the hogan, not an ideal solution, since many hogans are already crowded.

Then there is the ironing. Since there is no electricity, flat irons are used, and these must be heated on top of the stove or grate. Elsie and the other children, including the boys, take turns using the irons. They substitute a blanket-covered apple box for an ironing board, and do a remarkably good job of ironing their dresses and shirts.

How about fuel? It takes a great deal of wood even in the good weather, to keep the fires going; but in the winter time, particularly as was the case in this last severe winter, many families in our area had to buy their wood, which sells at $20.00 a quarter-ton truck load, or take the team and wagon, since none of my families owned cars or pickups, and travel quite long distances to obtain wood from the forests.

It takes Elsie and the children most of the weekend to get their clothes ready for the following school week. I suggest that when Elsie walks into her various high school classrooms, it is the rare teacher indeed who appreciates and understands what this girl has gone through in order to be the well-groomed and attractive young lady she is. It is no wonder that some mothers become discouraged and are not able to send their youngsters to school as immaculately as might be desired. Though the mothers I have met are remarkably cheerful, I have heard one or two complain that the job is just too much for them, particularly if the mother is not really "sold" on education and sees no real reason to expend that much effort in getting the children into the classrooms.

Elsie has other problems. She has homework to do, quite a lot of it. She gets home late, around dark in the winter time, and the kerosene lamp is already burning in the hogan. Because the mother is tired from herding the sheep and caring for the babies, Elsie does the cooking, and cooking the old Navajo way takes time, fried bread, fried potatoes, perhaps a mutton stew. Helping with dishes afterwards takes Elsie well into the evening. As is the habit of most Navajos in the winter time, the parents like to go to bed early. Even though the mother believes in education and sees to it that all of her children get to school, she does not always understand, especially since Elsie has been in school all day, why her daughter needs to sit up at night with her books. The younger children want to go to sleep, and there is the price of kerosene to be considered. So about the time Elsie can settle down to do her homework, everyone else in the hogan wants to blow out the lamp. Elsie, who ordinarily shows real respect for her parents and who enjoys a warmly affectionate relationship with them, said to me, "I feel so bad, because I tried to explain how I have to study, but they do not understand. So now I just act mean and refuse to blow out the lamp. I don't like to do like that." So Elsie shades the lamp chimney with a paper and gets her school work out of the way as quickly as possible (Green 1962:119-120).

The young Apache teen-ager aspiring to be a college graduate is setting his sights on a very unique achievement, for no Apache from the San Carlos reservation has in recent years graduated from a local college or university (Wesley 1961:4).* Thus, as far as educational achievement is concerned, there were no outstanding Apache adult models on the reservation for teen-agers to emulate.

According to the San Carlos Manpower Survey conducted by the Stanford Research Institute in 1954, the median number of school years completed was 8.2, as compared with 10.0 for the state of Arizona and 9.3 for the total United States (Robison et al. 1954:277). The point of this discussion is perhaps even better illustrated by comparing the SRI Report figures for college graduates. In the United States, 6.1% of the people had completed 4 or more years of college in 1950. In Arizona the figure for that year was 7.6%. The San Carlos Manpower Survey, however, found no Apaches having completed four years of college (Robison et al. 1954:277).

Bernardoni in 1962 attempted to uncover certain "critical factors" influencing the vocational choices of Apache teen-age boys from the Fort Apache Indian Reservation. He found the educational level of the parents interviewed to be only 6.8 years. Thus, the educational level of their high school children, the principal subjects of Bernardoni's research, was considerably higher than that of their parents. Seven of the parents admitted no formal education at all, and only two had graduated from high school, one having gone on to business college (Bernardoni 1962:4).

One result in this disparity of educational achievement

---

*A couple of Apache girls have obtained teaching degrees from mid-western Lutheran Mission colleges, and they were, at the time of this study, teaching in the Apache Lutheran Mission School system.

between Apache children and their parents, Bernardoni pointed out, was that:

> As the Apaches progressed through the grades, it became obvious that the students did not plan to utilize parental information or guidance in vocational plans but would inform their parents after they had made up their minds. None of the seniors felt that their parents could contribute much in vocational planning. . . . The Apache boys felt their parents are old-fashioned and would not understand their plans (Bernardoni 1962:5-6).

According to Bernardoni's Apache teen-agers, being uneducated is equated with being "old-fashioned," but for many adult Indians today, being called "old-fashioned," "backward," or "superstitious" simply means being Indian. There is considerable evidence to show that "being Indian"—that is to say, adhering to traditional tribal customs and beliefs—is a very important factor towards being accepted in an Indian community. Youngsters and even whole families find themselves strongly pressured into retaining prescribed Indian ways. As Wax points out in his discussion of Indian "conservatism," this has resulted in a kind of negativistic approach towards all aspects of the non-Indian culture, including formal education.

> As to proposals for current reform, the conservatives are thoroughly skeptical of anything issuing from the Whites or modeled upon them. In their judgment, the White is the alien, the enemy and the intruder, who has brought the Indian people only misery. "Acting White" is the most stinging epithet in their vocabulary. . . .
> The result is a negativism in which the energies of the conservative population are devoted to preserving a style of life that represents a sorry amalgam of impoverished White and deteriorated Indian cultures and with which they themselves are impatient. The more the administrators criticize and pressure for reform, the more they identify their true "Indianness" with the refusal to budge, even to improve their condition. (A good proportion of their White neighbors is ever happy to agree that the Indian cannot learn and will not change.) Their syndrome of economic impoverishment, isolation from other

cultures, and blind conservatism is self-reinforcing, and the greater the pressure upon them to change, the more they resist and withdraw (Wax 1963:695).

The late Grenville Goodwin wrote at length about the importance of the Apache system of social relationships and its concurrent effects on Apache economic and religious life. The keystone of this complex system of groups, bands, and clans was the *gotah* or family cluster: that is, several households living together through the mutual dependence of blood, clan, marital, and economic ties (Goodwin 1942:123). This form of the extended family system was a fundamental form of social unit that gave stability and security to its individual members, and persistence to many traditional Apache customs, i.e., the sharing of food and supplies, the raising of children within the framework of Apache cultural traditions, shelter and care for the aged, etc.

For the Apache child, the gotah was the basic social unit in which the process of socialization was institutionalized. It was the responsibility of certain adult members of this group to educate him about life and the surrounding environment, about ceremonial customs and religious beliefs, about marriage laws and social taboos—in other words, what it meant to be an Apache and how to act like one (Goodwin 1942: 461-480). More than just a die for the casting of individual character, the extended family was also ". . . the matrix of individual expression and activity" (Spicer 1962:473).

Today, the institution of the extended family has lost much of its former significance among the San Carlos Apache. According to Kaut, many Apache communities

> . . . appear to be in a state of rapid change. The present younger generation has lost touch with the old Apache way and has not yet found the new "American" or "indah" (enemy) way. Furthermore, the other Apache communities (outside of Cibecue) no longer seem to be organized according to the previously existing clan system (Kaut 1957:84).

While the traditional functions of the extended family system have by no means entirely died out, Apaches themselves admit that the number of gotahs has declined in recent years, and economic cooperation between families has become increasingly difficult. When Marinsek went into the field to study some of the effects of cultural differences in the education of Apache children in New Mexico—particularly among the Jicarilla and Mescaleros—he, too, found a diminishing importance in the obligatory ties that bind together the individuals of an extended family (Marinsek 1960:37).

The shifting of the economic base of Apache life to a cash and wage economy has caused the individual head of each nuclear family to act more independently of the other families. He is less likely to share his pay check with his wife's relatives because this is money he has earned himself which can be saved or spent at will to improve his family's housing, health, transportation, or education. Welfare and public health services have freed the family wage-earner considerably from the care of the sick and aged, while compulsory education has taken over a major portion of the family's responsibility towards the children. As families move to new areas on or off the reservation, where better living and working conditions prevail, many of the old gotahs have disintegrated, along with the complex of traditional Apache social customs that made them one of the most durable and significant of all the institutions contributing to the Apache way of life.

Unfortunately, as Marinsek (1960:38) points out: "With the changing structure of the family, concomitant social problems have developed. These include alcoholism, abandonment of children, gambling, and prostitution, all of which are evidences of the tensions inherent in a transitional culture." As the data will show, these social ills present a major stumbling-block to the Apache teen-ager attempting to achieve an education.

Changing sometimes at an even swifter pace than the traditional social structure of the reservation Indian was the nation-wide program of Indian education itself. In addition to the chronology of federal policy changes outlined in Chapter 1, there have been and continue to be gross inconsistencies in the formulation and operation of the various phases of the program. These came primarily out of the differing views of the administrators who promoted their own personal panaceas for the educational ills of the Indians.

One saw the solution in terms of improving personal dignity and motivation along with better community-school relationships (Orata 1953:205-215); another, in terms of communication and improving the methods for teaching English as a second language (Zintz 1960:136-137). Some raised the banner for more research without bothering to specify any vital areas (Thompson 1960:14-15), while yet another emphasized practical training for the increase of occupational success and the development of Indian natural and manpower resources (Beatty 1953:250).

Missionaries sought to strengthen the moral fiber of Indian youth, while public schools tried to prove that Indians were no different from non-Indians (Gonzales 1963:56-70). Just as some administrators were convinced of the need for more integrated schools in which Indians would be compelled to "comingle" with non-Indians (Head 1960:23-24), there were an equal number of Indians insistent about the need for more reservation community schools, where the Indian students could remain closer to home and their culture (Wauneka 1963:35).

This pulling and hauling within the general program of Indian Education at its various research and administrative centers had frequent repercussions at the local reservation levels. (In Chapter 4 these repercussions and their effects on the program of education for the San Carlos Apaches will be discussed in detail.) Ignorance played a major role in perpetrating these inconsistencies. Even after years of educating Indians, administrators still asked the question: "What makes these people tick?" (Parmee 1959-1961a:35). Teachers showed a rather shocking unawareness of Indian problems, which differed from those of the average non-Indian student. From Zintz's New Mexico study, we learn:

> . . . [Public school] teachers in general, are not sensitive to socio-cultural differences of Indian, Spanish-American, and Anglo children. While teachers were aware

of some rather obvious differences in language, customs and experience backgrounds, they did not interpret underlying value conflicts. . . . Equal educational opportunity is denied minority groups' children because the curriculum is geared to teachers' middle class, Anglo values. . . . These [minority group] children, in general, come from homes which have very limited understanding of the Anglo culture, much less the narrow segment of middle-class life style emphasized by the public school (Zintz 1960:106-109).

Of all the incongruities to be found throughout the program of education for Indians, the greatest has been the disparity between the elemental goals of the program as seen on the one hand by the educators, and on the other by many of the Indian people. In the first place, many Indians have been extremely suspicious of what they believe are rather covert, sinister Anglo aims behind the education program.

> . . . They feel that the schools are instrumentalities of the Whites, designed to inculcate Indian children with alien values and to transform them into "whites". . . . This notion of a threat to Indian identity poses the question of the extent to which conservative Indians feel that schools are punitively directed against their very being rather than designed to help them, as Indians, to improve their lot (Wax 1963:701).

In addition to this, says Zintz (1960:73): ". . . Indians may have considerable anxiety that the transfer of children to public schools, the move toward a money economy, and the conversion from extended to nuclear family living, are all steps toward the termination of services heretofore provided through the Bureau of Indian Affairs."

Thus, Indian parents have been known to evade cooperation with school officials, rather than express their fears and dislikes about some of the believed goals of the program. While a few may vent unfavorable feelings regarding major school issues or policies, such incidents are rare, and the majority simply offer a form of passive resistance. Efforts on the part of some Anglos to convince reticent Indians of the baselessness of their anxieties frequently fall on ears made deaf by a history of lies, corruption and faithless agreements.

Just as some Indians may have irrevocably negative convictions about the Anglo-sponsored school program, so have some educators evinced prejudices regarding the motives underlying the behavior of many Indians. The rather out-spoken research team of Murray and Rosalie Wax again struck hard at a sensitive issue when they attempted to illustrate this point in a recent *Journal of American Indian Education* article:

> At the upper levels of administration of the Pine Ridge (Sioux) Agency, Bureau ideology is now phrased as if it were a local variant of the national educational ideology of *cultural deprivation*. The Indian home and the mind of the Indian child are described as if they were empty or lacking in pattern. . . .
>
> Carried far enough, this Ideology of Cultural Deprivation leads to characterizations of Sioux life which are deplorably fallacious. . . .
>
> . . . Our own observations are that Bureau personnel are as hostile toward the Indians as the latter are toward them (and on both sides there are individuals who are not hostile); also, that Bureau personnel are utterly dependent upon the continued existence of the "backward" Indians, because if Indians managed their own affairs then the local Indian agency would provide no employment (this dependency is therefore especially among the lower and less skilled echelons of the Bureau). Our own observations again are that "apathy" is a convenient label to apply to people who don't happen to agree with the program that a government official or other reformer happens to be pushing (Wax and Wax 1964: 15, 16, 18).

The roots of these antagonisms between Anglos and Indians—or more accurately, between educators and some Indian families—are composed of a complex network of historical factors and present-day reservation conditions. The historical factors have already been touched upon: ruthless conquest by White settlers, degrading captivity on reservations, forced acculturation through boarding schools and dependency on federal services, and pervading this entire syndrome of relations with the White man, countless incidents in which deception, thievery, misunderstandings, and oppression by Anglos have made the Indian that much more the loser.

It is obvious that none of these things have helped Anglo-Indian relations, and on many reservations today communications between the people and official representatives of the two cultures are among the weakest of links in the rather tenuous chain that binds the two—if not in true friendship— at least in peaceful coexistence. This weakest of links has one of its most detrimental effects upon the program of Indian Education, for it is an area in which good faith, motivation, and mutual cooperation are essential to its success.

In their SSSP Monograph, Wax et al. described the problem of communication on the Pine Ridge Sioux Reservation:

> The Sioux community is isolated from the mainstream of national life and especially from the current where literacy and education are important and common. . . .
>
> Rarely do parents visit the schools and their classrooms. In turn, teachers rarely leave the school campus and the paved roads to observe any aspect of Sioux life. As a result, parents do not understand what their children should be doing or learning in school and, even when they wish to help their children obtain an education, they do not know what they might do to assist them. Conversely, most teachers know little about Sioux life and what little they know tends to repel them; thus they find it hard to reach out to their pupils (Wax, et al. 1964:102).

Robert L. Bennett and L. Madison Coombs (1964:25), respectively Juneau Area and Assistant Area directors for the Bureau of Indian Affairs, were apparently aware of this problem on Indian reservations today when they pointed out that:

> The education of native children and native adults, including the parents of the children, must go together. . . . Children cannot be educated successfully out of context with the understandings, expectations, and aspirations of their parents for them. . . . Our Bureau, and public school people as well, must do a better job than we have thus far done in interpreting to native parents

the specific reasons why a changing world will increasingly require more education for their children. . . . We have found that where there is a good adult education program the community interest in the school program for children almost invariably increases.

Bennett and Coombs expressed these views in 1964. When this study was being conducted, at a period prior to 1964, adult Indian Education programs were a rarity. In fact, today among the Indian tribes of Arizona, they are still a rarity. According to the 1964 Education Report of the Arizona Commission of Indian Affairs, only two of the sixteen reservations in the state had programs for adult education.

In the preceding pages an attempt has been made to discuss some of the more common problems in Indian education today, as found in the literature: i.e., social conflict, economic deprivation, and cultural instability. Going beyond this, however, these studies have also shown some of the serious personal psychological problems experienced by Indian children on reservations today. As Macgregor so vividly describes in his analysis of the development of the Dakota child personality:

> With the advent of puberty, the children begin to retire more completely within themselves and lose interest in the world around them. There is a decrease in their earlier spontaneity and freedom of behavior. The restraint set up by environmental pressures now appears to take complete control. The personalities of the adolescents seem not to mature; they appear to resign themselves, to become apathetic and passive, and to accept the anxiety the outer world creates. In the fact of this empty and unfriendly world, the adolescents and post-adolescents become still more frightened and retricted.
>
> . . . Dakota child personality seems crippled and negative, as if it rejected life. The unfriendly environment, which offers so little opportunity or satisfaction, retards the growth of personality and prevents it from becoming positive, rich and mature. Life is lived on the defensive (Macgregor 1946:208-209).

Considering the disheartening community conditions described in the literature for many of today's Indian reservations, and considering the unquestionably detrimental effects these conditions have on the personal growth and maturation of the Indian child as he or she struggles to compete in the distinctly Anglo-oriented program of education to which he is committed, the social and academic problems of Apache teen-agers described in the two succeeding chapters should come as no surprise to the reader.

CHAPTER 3

The Problems of Apache Youth in School

FOR MORE THAN TEN YEARS, Apache students living on the San Carlos Reservation have been exposed to three major types of school systems: federal, public, and mission schools, with separate schools operating independently within each system.

I. *Public Schools:*
    a) Globe School District (serving the San Carlos community) (206)*
        1) East Globe Elementary—Apaches attending grades 5 and 6
        2) Hill Street Jr. High—Apaches attending grades 7 and 8
        3) Globe High School—Apaches attending grades 9-12
    b) Ft. Thomas School District (serving the Bylas community) (121)
        1) Ft. Thomas Elementary — Apaches attending grades 1-6
        2) Ft. Thomas Jr. High and High School—Apaches attending grades 7-12
    c) Rice School District (serving the San Carlos community) (50)
        1) Rice Public School—Apaches attending grades 1-4

*The figures in ( ), denoting Apache student enrollment, were compiled during the winter of the 1959-60 school year from current school records. These figures varied throughout the school year because of mid-year transfers.

II. *Federal Schools:*
   a) Reservation Day Schools: (426)
      1) San Carlos Day School—Apaches attending grades Beginners-4
      2) Bylas Day School—Apaches attending grades Beginners-4
   b) Off-Reservation Boarding Schools: (184)
      1) Phoenix Indian School—Apaches eligible to attend grades 7-12
      2) Stewart Indian School—Apaches eligible to attend tend grades 7-12
      3) Theodore Roosevelt Boarding School—Apaches eligible to attend grades 1-8
      4) Sherman Institute—Apaches eligible to attend grades 1-12

III. *Mission Schools:*
   a) Reservation Day Schools (152)
      1) Peridot Lutheran Mission School—teaching grades 1-12
      2) Bylas Lutheran Mission School—teaching grades 1-12
   b) Off-Reservation Boarding Schools (65)
      1) East Fork Lutheran Mission School—teaching grades 1-12
      2) St. John's Catholic Mission School — teaching grades 5-12
      3) Southwest Indian School (Glendale Mission School)—teaching grades 1-12

The federal reservation day schools were owned and operated by the Bureau of Indian Affairs, Branch of Education. The local reservation principal maintained an office at the San Carlos BIA Agency and functioned as a kind of school superintendent, overseeing the programs of each individual federal school on the reservation. These schools, one each at San Carlos and Bylas at the time, were separately staffed with a school principal, teachers, custodians, bus drivers, and cafeteria workers.

Tribal law required all Apache children to enter school at least by the age of six. At this age, most enrolled in the two federal reservation day schools, where "Beginners" classes were held to teach the non-English-speaking Apache children some rudiments of English, and to acquaint them with the basic patterns of school life. After the fourth grade, however, students were transported each day to the off-reservation public schools at Globe or Ft. Thomas, or they were sent directly to any one of a number of federal boarding schools, far from the reservation environs.

One of the primary responsibilities of the reservation principal was to select eligible Apache students for boarding schools. At San Carlos the applications, usually submitted by the family of each child, had to have the approval of the BIA social worker, the reservation principal, and the agency superintendent. Briefly summarized, the criteria for the selection of boarding school enrollees was stated as follows:

Education Criteria:

1) no other school is available
2) where special vocational or preparatory courses are necessary
3) scholastically retarded students, or those with severe bilingual problems

Social Criteria:

1) neglected or rejected children
2) children from inadequate home environments
3) children with extreme behavior problems
4) children whose health is jeopardized by the illness of household members

(Bureau of Indian Affairs 1956:2)

Each federal boarding school had its own special education programs, ranging from the academic to the more vocational aspects of training. Each was run by a separate administrative and teaching staff, and operated independently from reservation directives. Coordination between the federal boarding schools and the federal reservation education system was managed through annual conferences of school administrators, and supervised through the Washington and regional area offices. Most of the federal boarding schools provided academic and vocational training up through the twelfth grade.

Upon fulfillment of the fourth grade requirements, however, most Apache youngsters remained at home, to be transported daily to the off-reservation public schools. At the time of this study, these schools were owned and operated by the local district tax payers, who lived off the reservation, and who were for the most part non-Indians. The schools functioned after the pattern of many Arizona public schools, with elected school boards (all non-Indians in 1961) functioning independently from any reservation authority. Criticism from BIA officials, however, was usually keenly attended to because the overwhelming majority of funds for the support of the Apache children in the public schools came as a result of federal legislation, over which higher BIA echelons had some influence.

Globe Public Schools provided a part-time guidance counselor for Indian students. It was his job to help with the adjustment of the Indian students into the school routine by providing extra attention and extra assistance when necessary. At Ft. Thomas, the smaller of the two public school systems, the high school principal devoted a part of his time to the problems of the Indian students to make up for the lack of a special counselor.

Remedial reading courses were established in both school programs and many Apaches were encouraged to take them. Federal subsidies provided free lunches to all Indian students in public school, but high school Indian students had to purchase their own books and supplies as did all non-Indians. However, assistance from a variety of sources was usually found for needy cases through the cooperation of public, federal, and tribal agencies.

The mission schools had another education program of their own. In addition to the day schools at Bylas and Peridot, the Lutherans also maintained a boarding school at East Fork on the Ft. Apache Reservation. Catholic Apaches wishing to send their children to a parochial school usually sent them to St. John's Indian School in Laveen, Arizona, for there were no Catholic mission day schools on the San Carlos Reservation. At the time of this study, however, hopes were high among parishioners that a school would be built in the foreseeable future.

Contact between the mission schools and the other two

school systems was limited. The strict policy of church and state separation prohibited federal aid to the mission school program, even to the extent that needy mission students found it difficult to get assistance for books and clothing. As federal aid to public education increased over the years, Apache parents found it advantageous to transfer their children from the mission schools in order to get money for educational expenses.

In the spring of 1958, prior to this study, the San Carlos tribal chairman appointed his newly elected vice-chairman to head the tribal education committee. By this action it was hoped that new impetus would be given to what BIA officials saw as a growing Apache interest in the education of their people.* It was the purpose of this committee to:

1) encourage parental interest in education by acting as a sounding-board for complaints and providing useful assistance, e.g., educational loans

2) sponsor constructive extra-curricular activities for Apache students, and other educational projects, e.g., local newspaper

3) help coordinate different programs of educational aid to parents and children, e.g., Save the Children Federation

4) inform agencies of control, such as the tribal council, BIA education offices, public schools, etc., of the people's needs.

5) inform the people of new programs, regulations, and benefits provided for educational purposes by the controlling agencies

The Apache tribal council also provided the services of one or more juvenile officers to combat truancy and delinquency and to counsel with parents and students experiencing educational difficulties. Since their appointment to this position was generally based upon an ability to get along with children and a position of high regard among Apaches and Anglos alike, these officers were frequently called upon to assist in matters where the normal Anglo channels of communication had failed.

This completes a review of the major components in the

---

*From a conversation with the BIA reservation superintendent.

program of Apache education.* A critical analysis of their contributions to this program will come later in a more specific discussion of problems and underlying causes. The following section will deal with some of the indices that were used in this study to measure the relative success—or failure—of Apache students to respond to formal education as it was presented between 1959 and 1961.

School Enrollment, 1949-1961

Available records† for this twelve year period indicated that the enrollment of Apache school-age children remained well above the 90% mark. From this standpoint, at least, it can be said that the school program had been successful in reaching out into nearly every household on the reservation. This was not true twenty or thirty years ago when many Apache parents hid their children from the school disciplinary officer who came to take them away to boarding school.

This high rate of school enrollment among Apache children was due to at least two factors, revealed from the observations and interviews of this study:

1) There was a growing willingness on the part of most Apache parents to have their children enrolled in school; and

2) there was a persistent effort on the part of Anglo and Indian reservation officials to see that the streets were kept free of delinquent school children.

The greater part of the small minority of unenrolled Apache school-age children was found to consist primarily of drop-outs, for whom school work had become such an impossibility that much of the academic year was lost and would have to be repeated.

---

*It should be noted here that the tiny Rice Public School at San Carlos has been omitted from this discussion. This is because it played a rather insignificant role in the education of Apaches. It was a school maintained primarily for the convenience of San Carlos BIA agency personnel, who did not care to send their grammar school children into Globe because of the long bus ride each day. BIA personnel were not allowed to enroll their children in the local federal school. Rice School at Gilson Wash was finally closed down in 1961 when San Carlos Day School was turned into a cooperative federal-public school.

†Combined BIA Agency and project reports.

Attitudes toward the enrollment of Beginners (pre-first graders) were indicative of the overall feeling on the part of Apache parents and school officials about school enrollment. In 1960 it was rare indeed to find a primary school-age Apache child roaming freely out of school for any length of time. More frequently than not, such an occurence happened through an oversight or error in the agency records rather than through intentional resistance on the part of the parents. As soon as the error was discovered, it was swiftly corrected and the child was enrolled in school. Thus, by keeping in contact with reservation families through the variety of tribal, BIA, and U.S. Public Health services, and by maintaining an up-to-date census record of the total population, school officials were able to keep close tabs on all potential students.

Most Apache children, however, upon reaching school age, seldom got the chance to play hooky. Many Apache parents sought to enroll their children as soon as possible, and for some the six year age limit for Beginners in federal schools was frequently a source of aggravation. These parents preferred to have their children begin this pre-primary grade at five years, the same age as non-Indian children. In fact, this observer interviewed some parents who felt so strongly about this that they made a special effort to enroll their five year olds in public and mission schools where limited facilities made admission difficult, rather than in the large federal reservation day schools where most Apache children began their education.

With Apaches involved in three separate systems of education, it is important to compare the trends in enrollment for each of the systems in order to understand where some of the primary school problems existed. As can be seen from the above chart, the relative proportions of Apache enrollment in public, federal, and mission schools changed considerably during the twelve year period from 1949 to 1961.

Whereas in 1949 the great majority of Apache students (69.3%) were attending federally operated day and boarding schools, the proportion of Apaches in both federal and public schools was almost equal by 1959, ten years later. Mission school enrollment increased only slightly between the years

San Carlos Apaches in Public, Federal And Mission Schools, 1949-1961

Comparative Percentages of Total Enrollment

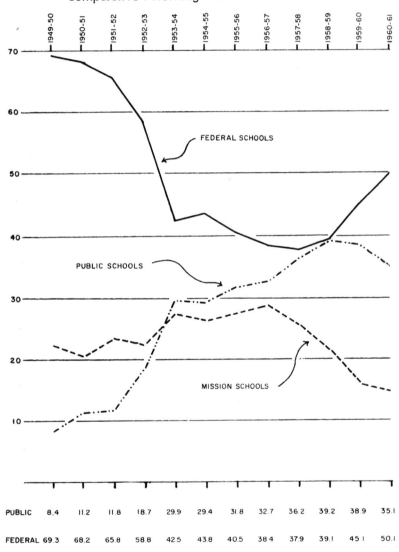

PUBLIC	8.4	11.2	11.8	18.7	29.9	29.4	31.8	32.7	36.2	39.2	38.9	35.1
FEDERAL	69.3	68.2	65.8	58.8	42.5	43.8	40.5	38.4	37.9	39.1	45.1	50.1
MISSION	22.2	20.6	23.2	22.4	27.5	26.1	27.6	28.8	25.8	21.6	16.0	14.8

(SOURCES: B.I.A. ANNUAL SCHOOL CENSUS REPORTS FROM THE SAN CARLOS AGENCY)

1949 to 1954, but this period did witness a tremendous shift in enrollment between the federal and public schools, as the federal reservation day schools liquidated their upper grades and the children moved into public off-reservation day schools primarily at Globe and Ft. Thomas. Between 1954 and 1959, the enrollment in federal schools continued to decline as the public school rolls increased, until by 1959—as has been mentioned—their respective shares of the entire student population were almost equal. The mission schools reached their peak in 1956 with 28.8% of the total, but after 1957 they experienced a sharp reduction in students. The enrollment in public schools also declined after 1959, as federal school enrollment increased.

The principal factors influencing these trends appeared to be circumstantial rather than preferential as far as Apaches were concerned. In the 1950's federal policies towards Indians, as previously stated in Chapter 1, were in favor of assimilating all Indians into the greater Anglo society. The situation described by the twelve year survey presented here shows a clear example of the implementation of these policies.

Between 1949 and 1953 the Bureau of Indian Affairs decided to close down its community high schools at Bylas and San Carlos in favor of the integration policies of Washington lawmakers. Since integration could not be achieved to any notable extent within reservation boundaries because there were so few White children living there, the off-reservation public school systems at Globe and Ft. Thomas were requested to accept Apache students. Money provided by the Johnson-O'Malley Act of 1936 was used to help the public schools offset their increased expenses brought on by this sudden rise in enrollment.*

Between 1953 and 1955 a further step was taken to increase the proportion of Apaches in public schools, when the 7th and 8th grades at San Carlos and Bylas were eliminated. Finally, in 1957, the 5th and 6th grades were closed out and sent to off-reservation public schools. From that year until

---

*For a complete discussion of the Johnson-O'Malley Act provisions, see the report of the Arizona Commission of Indian Affairs, *Federal and State Participation in Indian Education*, 1961-1962, Phoenix, pp. 14-18.

1961, only the first five years of school—Beginners through 4th grade—remained active on the reservation at Bylas and San Carlos in the federal day schools.

Although the mission schools never achieved more than 28% of the total student enrollment during the twelve year period, they did experience a decline after 1956. There is reason to believe that this decline can be attributed in part to the rising influence of the Pentacostal churches at that time. As the popularity of this new kind of religion grew, the older reservation missions, sponsored by the Lutherans and the Catholics, began to lose their parishioners. Support of the mission schools was costly, since they did not enjoy federal and state assistance. Lutheran mission policymakers finally decided that only the children of their most loyal parishioners could attend the mission schools, and as a result, some students were compelled to go elsewhere.

It would be misleading to conclude from the high enrollment figures stated that school enrollment per se was no longer a problem for the San Carlos Apaches. An analysis of attendance records (see below) showed that mid-year transfers were prevalent throughout the entire program. This was discovered when efforts to compile complete individual student attendance records for the 1959-60 school year were thwarted by so many incomplete school records. For example, a child would enroll in one day school in September, then transfer to boarding school in November. After the Christmas holidays, his name might again show up on the rolls of the previous day school, where—perhaps—he would finish out the year.

This erratic migration of students was enough to disrupt a sizeable number of individual student attendance records, but no exact figure could be determined for transfers alone. Nevertheless, for whatever the reason—transfers, dropouts, or data errors—it can be said that during the 1959-60 school year, 392 out of 1174 students enrolled in day schools did not complete their year's study at the school in which they were originally enrolled.*

The observations of the author, while working with school

---

*Apache enrollment figures for 1959-60 are listed in ( ) on pages 24, 25 and 26.

officials in various capacities, tended to support the statistical evidence above. Several times each week, the reservation principal was confronted by some unhappy parent or student seeking a transfer from one school to another. Parents having disciplinary problems with their children at home would seek to have them sent to boarding school. Students experiencing difficulty in adjusting to one school would ask to be sent to another. Families seeking employment off the reservation, wherever and whenever it was available, would take their children with them. Mid-year transfers were not only indicative of student problems, but the high rate of such transfers was also a recognizable factor in contributing to the failure of many to meet the expected academic standards for educational progress.

Daily Attendance in School

By their very nature boarding schools tended to eliminate any attendance problems. Apache teen-agers enrolled in such schools had little opportunity to play hooky in such a highly controlled environment where teachers, supervisors and a variety of counselors and attendants were continually watching over their students. The few who did manage to elude supervision, or who openly defied it, were swiftly and firmly reprimanded. Thus, the discussion of Apache teen-age attendance will be based primarily on public high school records.*

Public school officials at Globe and Ft. Thomas kept monthly attendance records for Apache students primarily because of the need to present daily enrollment totals each year to the federal government for cost reimbursement through the Johnson-O'Malley program. From these materials, the research staff of this study compiled individual student attendance records for every Apache enrolled 150 days or more in the same school during the 1959-60 school year. Interviews with teachers and school officials assisted in the formulation of an "attendance scale" to which the completed individual rec-

---

*The small number of Apache teen-age students attending the mission day schools does not warrant the inclusion of their figures in the data presented here, nor will their exclusion in any way change the validity of the findings.

ords could be applied. This scale consisted of the following categories:

1) Perfect Attendance: 0.0% absence for the year
2) Good Attendance: 0.1-4.9% absence for the year, or up to 1 day's absence every 4 weeks
3) Fair Attendance: 5.0-9.9% absence for the year, or up to 2 days' absence every 4 weeks
4) Danger Zone: 10.0-14.9% absence for the year, or up to 3 days' absence every 4 weeks
5) Poor Attendance: 15.0-19.9% absence for the year, or up to 1 day's absence every week
6) Inadequate Attendance for Normal Scholastic Progress: includes all categories of 20% absence for the year or higher. Most students missing 1 day a week from school or more were considered unlikely to be able to keep up with the rest of the class in school.

At Globe High School, the records showed that 68% of the enrolled (150 days or more) Apache students had either "Fair" or "Good" attendance records, while the remaining 32% had records falling in categories 4, 5, and 6, indicating definite attendance problems. At Ft. Thomas High School, meanwhile, only 47% of the enrolled Apache students had records in the upper three categories. The remaining 53% were missing school to a degree beyond what most teachers and administrators considered to be adequate for normal academic progress.

School officials—both Indian and non-Indian—blamed the higher absence rate among Bylas teen-agers primarily on the accessability of liquor in the Geronimo area, just between Bylas and Ft. Thomas. More than likely, a combination of factors contributed to the problem: 1) reduced recreational facilities within the Bylas community resulting from the loss of the local day school facilities, 2) a greater degree of poverty in Bylas than in San Carlos (although this was apparent, it has yet to be actually proven), and 3) the easy accessibility of liquor to both adults and minors.

By lumping the records of the Apaches from both schools,

it can be seen that 42.5% of public high school Apaches missed
2 days or more out of every 20 days of classes: 17.5% missed
2-3 days out of every 20, 9% missed 3-4 days, and 12%
missed 4-5 days. Eight per cent of the Apache students at Ft.
Thomas High School (none from Globe) missed more than
one fourth of the entire academic year. It is also important to
note that the enrollment of Apaches in government boarding
schools reached an all-time high in 1959-60. This meant that
a sizable number of problem cases had been removed from the
reservation; had they been in public school, the attendance
records for the year would very likely have been much worse.

The extent of the teen-age Apache attendance problem
in the off-reservation public schools must also be considered
in the light of other factors:

1) Apache high school students in the main were not
   habitual attendance problems as some school officials
   at the time believed they were. No less than 67.2%
   of these students had adequate attendance for the
   year. A few even had perfect attendance records at
   Ft. Thomas High School. The problem, then, was not
   one of rampant proportions; it was limited to an
   unmistakable core of "repeaters," whose problems
   were such that they caused the continual interruption
   of schooling by incurring a high rate of absenteeism.
2) Additional attendance data showed definite trends in
   the rate of absenteeism. In the on-reservation government day schools for example, where the majority (ap-
   prox. 340 in 1959-60) of Apache youngsters obtained
   their schooling up through the fourth grade, as much
   at 76% of the students had adequate attendance for
   the year. Some 36 students, in fact, had perfect attendance records. Those Apaches in the public
   schools, however, the majority of whom were in
   grades 5 through 8, had the smallest percentage of
   adequate attendance (56%) for the year.

When used in conjunction with the interview and scholastic data, these differing percentages revealed some understand-

ing of the intensity of school and personal-social Apache problems at different academic and age levels. It seemed evident that those Apache students leaving the reservation day schools to enter grades 5, 6, 7, and 8 at Globe and Ft. Thomas experienced considerable difficulty in adjusting socially and academically to the new, integrated public school system. These problems, combined with their own adolescent growing pains made them the most susceptible to absenteeism.

At the high school level, many of these students continued to suffer from the problems compounded in the lower grades, and their attendance records were indicative of these difficulties in the presence of a more demanding curriculum. Sources in the literature also tend to support this interpretation (Zintz 1960:75 and Boyce 1960:5).

During the interviews with high school Apache students, specific questions were asked about the transition between the on-reservation BIA schools and the public schools. The answers varied. Some students said that they did not like going to the public schools at first because they felt very much in the minority. The non-Indian students appeared cold and unfriendly, and the teachers seemed to pay more attention to the non-Indians.

Other Apache high school students admitted that the sudden change was quite a shock at first, primarily because the classwork was much harder, the competition was greater, and homework was required for the first time. These Apache students had no complaints about their non-Indian peers, other than the fact that they were tough competitors.

All of the high school interviewees remarked about the sudden increase in the educational demands from their teachers when first entering the public schools, but some claimed that they became accustomed to it. Their greatest difficulty, they said, was communication. Not only was it hard to keep up with the pace of the teacher's instructions, but some recalled having difficulty understanding the chatter of their fellow classmates on the playground. This discouraged a number of Apaches from making a greater effort to learn English. During recess, many stayed with groups of their own kind and spoke Apache, experiencing perhaps for the first time the somber reality of their own uniqueness.

3) Perhaps one of the most surprising results from the analysis of attendance was the realization that there was no consistent correlation between good attendance and good scholastic achievement. While poor attendance nearly always coincided with a variety of academic problems and low scholastic achievement, there were also Apache students in the higher grade levels with outstanding daily attendance rates who were doing very poorly in school.

Interviews with some of the public school teachers revealed that such students merely sat in class, physically present, but apparently mentally out of step with the pace of the rest of the class. Their response to classwork and home assignments was barely minimal and at the end of the year they were either held back in class, or if over-aged, "socially promoted" to the next grade. The teachers themselves were baffled as to why such students bothered to come to school regularly in the face of such hopeless prospects. But these were generally the more submissive types of Apache children, who remained stoically silent in the classroom, seldom caused any trouble in school, and who persistently refused to communicate any difficulties to their teachers.

During the fall of 1959, when the author and his interpreter had an opportunity to aid the tribal juvenile officer with his truancy and house-to-house counseling chores, many of the reasons underlying the absentee problem came to light. Several months later, when this particular phase of the project had come to an end, hundreds of homes in the San Carlos and Peridot communities had been visited and personal contacts made with occupant families. The following is a discussion of some of the more significant findings.

THE "PROBLEM CASES": FAMILY ENVIRONMENT AS A FACTOR IN ABSENTEEISM

The real, so-called "problem cases" comprised a distinct group, a rather constant number who had to be visited time and time again. These students made up about 40% of the total student population but they required a far greater proportion of counseling time, for communication was frequently difficult and good rapport was hard to achieve. The problem seemed not so much one of language as of values and ideas, as well as a basic lack of mutual understanding between the students, their parents, and those in charge of the education program. Out of these families a number of characteristic "types" emerged.

The "skid-row" family

Families of this type comprised as much as 21% of the sample 100 cases. Counseling with these families very often left one with a feeling of hopelessness. Broken marriages, drinking, moral degeneration, poverty, and complacency were but a few of the obstacles that confronted the counselor and affected the lives of the Apache children belonging to these families. Since many such families had been on "skid-row" for years, hours and hours of repeated talks could do little to alleviate their situation.

In numerous cases the children from these families were hustled off to boarding school to begin what was hoped to be a new and more constructive way of life, assumed feasible in the controlled daily environment found there. But the "skid-row" parents and relatives remained behind, to haunt their children with unhappy letters and phone calls and to prey upon them once again during the summer vacation months. It was not unusual to hear bitter objections from the children of such families when they were forced to return home—perhaps a misnomer—for the summer. Such cases prompted tribal leaders to develop a summer camp program to offer needy students a more stable and constructive environment for at least part of each summer.

The "sympathetic" family

In such families it was not unusual to find financially well-to-do parents or relatives. One of the dominant characteristics of the sympathetic family seemed to be a strong, somewhat domineering mother or grandmother who sided with her children in almost every dispute. The children of such families generally grew up in an atmosphere of economic stability and social solidarity. Along with the characteristically traditional Apache female authority went a style of family life that was also more traditional.

Hostile attitudes towards the school program, the Bureau of Indian Affairs, or towards Anglos in general often came to light when counseling with families of this nature. Old, bitter memories of unhappy experiences added much fuel to their complaints. It should be noted, however, that occasionally when it was possible to patch-up wounded feelings and clear up any misunderstandings, cooperation in school matters from these families could generally be relied upon because of the strong backing of the elder in authority who diligently sought after the welfare of the family. Even the most traditionally-oriented Apache elder confronted by the author was not opposed to education, but rather to the manner in which it was implemented.

"Weak-authority" families

In such families discipline of the delinquent or unruly child was extremely difficult, for unlike the "sympathetic" family, there was no stable authoritarian figure present. Cooperation in family or school matters prevailed only on occasions of mutual consent between the child and his elders.* Conditions such as these often existed in families where there were weak or infirm foster parents, or a helpless widow or divorcee. It was not unusual for an elder in this family to request the aid of some outside authority to help discipline his or her children. The relationship of current Apache disciplinary practices to community law and order enforcement will be discussed later at some length.

In summing up this presentation of the teen-age "problem cases," a category which included the worst attendance offenders, it can be said that the unfortunate nature of the family conditions contributed significantly to the problems of the individual children. Consideration of any solutions to these

---

*While many Apache parents, unlike some Anglos, preferred not to interfere with their children's behavior and attitudes, even the most tolerant parents resorted to firm disciplinary measures when they judged the matter too serious to be overlooked.

problems, therefore, necessarily had to include at the very start ways for solving the overriding family difficulties.

The reasons given by Apache parents and children for absenteeism were many, but the most prominent of all was "illness." Checking out the absences that were reportedly due to illness uncovered a number of interesting points that indicated some possible differences between Anglos and Apaches. There were, of course, occasions when illness was used as an excuse to cover up the real reasons for the student's absence, but the author's Apache interpreter was usually both clever and honest enough to distinguish such cases from the rest, which were, from the Apache viewpoint, perfectly legitimate cases of illness.

During certain periods of the school year many Apache children, in all age groups and especially those from poverty-stricken homes, became ill. Respiratory illness, trachoma (particularly in the lower grades), and various types of bacterial infections were the most common, causing many absences from school.

Prior to 1961, when Public Health, BIA and tribal services stepped in to improve the situation, the average Apache home consisted of a one-, two-, or three-room house of wood construction with no indoor water and sanitation facilities, no insulation, and only the necessary minimum in heating units: either a wood or kerosene stove. Though the climate could be extremely warm in the summer, temperatures were not infrequently below freezing in winter. Infectious diseases, particularly colds and flu, were prevalent during the winter months, often exhibiting a rapid spread throughout the student population.

It was also not unusual to find a child staying home with what appeared to be only minor discomforts, such as a sore limb or headache, that for most Anglo parents and school officials would not have constituted a legitimate excuse for absence. Apaches, however, generally disagreed with such a viewpoint. In their eyes, such aches and pains were possibly symptomatic of a serious malady, either physical or emotional.

The best remedy was to keep the child at home, comfort him, and watch for any developments. Trying to argue with a parent on the grounds that a simple aspirin would alleviate what was "probably a minor, temporary discomfort" only convinced him or her of your lack of real concern for the child's welfare.

Talking with Apache mothers about illness and disease soon revealed that very few really understood the theory of germs and the fundamentals of modern home medical care. Though few admitted adherence to traditional Apache cures, such as herbs, parts of animals, magic talismans, and cere- monial cures (King 1954: 22), traditional views regarding the phenomenon of illness itself appeared common.

1) Aside from certain recognizable illnesses clearly de- fined by Anglo doctors—the common cold, trachoma, etc.— less easily identifiable illnesses were thought by Apaches to be the result of some previous violation of traditional Apache religious beliefs or even witchcraft.

2) Fear itself was a kind of illness (Opler 1946: 22) that was believed to be caused by some evil influence. Young children were particularly susceptible and had to be frequently cared for at home by their mothers for this ailment.

3) Illnesses that did not appear to respond to treatment from the local public health doctor were considered to be extremely serious, and probably of spiritual origin. The parent of a child afflicted in this manner might then turn to a respected gotah leader for advice, or go directly to a medicine man. Apaches normally did not expect Anglos to understand or appreciate the seriousness of such illnesses; consequently, the use of traditional cures was almost never discussed with Anglos.*

A certain degree of unfamiliarity with the medical care

---

*On one unique occasion the author was approached by a close Apache friend and in secrecy asked if he thought a daughter of his could be cured by a medicine man. The daughter was having serious social adjustment problems. "Everyone has tried in every way to help her," he said, "but nothing seems to help. She won't listen to anyone. It's just like she's crazy in the head, or something. Some people say she's 'witched' and we should take her to a medicine man. But some people don't believe in that kind of stuff any more. What do you think?" My answer was honest but ambiguous. Not being an Apache, I said, made it difficult for me to advise him in such matters. My views might be biased. I told him to speak to some older men of his tribe.

provided in school for the needs of every child, coupled with the basic conviction that no teacher or school administrator could possibly have the concern for an ailing Apache child the way its mother could, gave most Apache parents ample cause for keeping a sick child home from school. Even among parents who openly professed the importance of education, this strong, protective feeling about their children predominated. Considering the high death rate among Indian children until a few years ago, particularly among infants,* Apache parents might well have had good reason to be so concerned (Goodwin 1942: 453).

MISUNDERSTANDINGS AS A CAUSE FOR ABSENTEEISM

Again and again simple misunderstandings were found to be responsible for absenteeism. A high school teen-ager, for example, might come home one afternoon with a problem, perhaps a request of some sort from the school. Since in most Apache families, children were not asked about their daily activities—and few volunteered information on their own—the problem might not come to light until the next morning when it was time to prepare for school. Then the student would voice a bitter complaint against the school and beg to be kept at home for fear of punishment by some teacher or administrator. Unable to cope with the problem at such short notice, or perhaps unable to understand it fully, the puzzled parent, fearing for the safety of the child, kept the child at home.

Counseling with the parent and child revealed in almost every case a rather limited understanding of the facts surrounding the incident and, on the part of the parent, an even more limited understanding of school procedures and policies in general. Usually the incomplete or distorted information that the child had to offer was all that the parent had on which to base his or her decision. The student may have misunderstood the teacher's request, or the teacher may have misunderstood the student's reason for having difficulty in fulfilling that request. This misunderstanding was further complicated when presented to the unknowing parents by the student; and a

---

*Indian infant mortality rate in mid-1950's was 275 per 1000 births. U.S. population figures were 28 per 1000 births.

situation resulted which was sufficient for at least one day's absence, and possibly more if not attended to that day.

A prompt clearing of the confusion through the aid and diplomacy of the tribal juvenile officer seldom failed to get the child back in school immediately. Often further problems of a similar nature were avoided because of the brief learning experience provided the parent through a counseling session.

THE EFFECTS OF SHAME AND SCHOOL DISCIPLINE ON ABSENTEEISM

It was not unusual to find an Apache child at home because an unhappy incident in school had caused him to feel embarrassed and ashamed. Such incidents created highly emotional situations necessitating the most sensitive handling on the part of the counselor or intermediary. They occurred most frequently in the integrated public schools, where old racial antagonisms and poor family-school communications tended to complicate and distort the real issues at hand. The inevitable misunderstandings were difficult to iron out under such conditions, and as often as not the outcome would find the angry and humiliated parents insisting on transferral of their child to another school. The following actual incident should help to illustrate this discussion.

Emily Alberta (fictitious name) was progressing in public school, until one day she was sent home with the report that she had lice in her hair. Her family was quite embarrassed, and Emily was scrubbed well and sent back to school. Again she returned home with a notice of the same complaint. Only this time she was told not to return to school until she had rid herself of all the lice.

The parents were incensed, and reported the incident to the reservation principal and the social worker. Emily refused to go back to school under any circumstances, and her parents were strongly in sympathy. Several phone calls clarified the problem, and a Public Health Nurse was sent to the home to eradicate the source of the girl's reinfection.

In a week's time, after much coaxing, the Albertas finally agreed to send Emily back to school. She returned home once more with word from the school nurse, claiming that there were "indications" of lice still in her hair. An examination by the PHS doctor refuted this claim, and the reservation principal unleashed a vigorous protest against the public school officials. No amount of apologies, however could soften the hearts of Emily's irate parents, and in a short time she was sent away to boarding school.

A thorough investigation of the causes behind unfortunate incidents like this one brought to light factors which created the conditions fostering misunderstandings. Anglo teachers and school administrators were generally ignorant of Apache disciplinary methods—in fact, many believed that Apache parents did not discipline their children at all—and unknowingly used their own methods of reprimand, shaming the Apache student, sometimes before the eyes of his classmates. This left the student open to ridicule and disapproval, particularly from non-Indian peers.

Traditionally, public disapproval and ridicule have been used by Apaches as strong corrective measures for teen-agers and adults alike: measures which were "feared and avoided above everything" (Goodwin 1942:459). The use of such methods by school personnel for minor infractions was considered by Apaches to be unjustly harsh and discriminatory.

Anglo teachers, insensitive or ignorant of the competition between Apache and non-Apache students (with the former usually feeling somewhat inferior), would create emotional crises that often hindered Apache students in their efforts to adjust to the integrated school program.

SEASON AS A FACTOR IN ABSENTEEISM

By plotting the monthly rate of absenteeism, it was discovered that at certain times of the school year Apache students were more prone to absenteeism than at other times. September, October, January, and March had the highest incidence of absences, while December, February, April, and May had the lowest. Investigation, not entirely conclusive, pointed to the following probable causes:

1) September and October found Apache students experiencing their most difficult period of adjustment to the new year

of class routine, new teachers, perhaps higher levels of work, and perhaps a new school altogether. Homesickness was felt most strongly during this time.

2) By November and December most students had settled down to their routine of schoolwork, and newly-made friendships eased the pangs of homesickness.

3) In January some students, having enjoyed their Christmas vacation, refused to return to school on a regular basis. Faced with semester exams, some made an effort to drop out of school entirely.

4) February saw the beginning of the new semester with some of the more serious attendance offenders either in boarding school or out of school entirely.

5) With the coming of warm, spring-like weather in March, hooky-playing at times got quite out of hand; but by April and May this was under control.

6) Illness was most prevalent during the months of October, January, and March.

SCHOLASTIC PROBLEMS AS A FACTOR IN ABSENTEEISM

Along with the above factors influencing the annual rate of absenteeism among Apache students—family environment, illness, poor communications and misunderstandings, school disciplinary practices, and time of year—scholastic difficulties created problems which often led to reluctance on the part of some Apaches to stay in school. This was a particularly influential factor at the higher grade levels where the school work was more demanding and the work loads were heavier. Many Apaches at these grade levels were in the integrated public schools, and competing academically with non-Indians having a background of cultural experiences more in line with the curriculum of the public school system accentuated many of their scholastic problems.

Academic Achievement in School

In measuring the scholastic achievement of teen-age Apache students, a number of criteria were used: intelligence tests comparing Indians with non-Indians, a comparison of Indian and non-Indian grade averages, the incidence of Apache age-grade lag in the upper grade levels, social promotions in the public schools, and the Apache teen-age drop-out rate.

Before discussing any one of these criteria, however, a few remarks regarding the various techniques used are in order.

In a project of this size it was impossible to investigate all the phases of the program of education for Apaches on the basis of the total school population. The data had to be gathered in areas where it was most feasible and at times when it best suited the convenience of each individual school. For each of the criteria discussed below, however, a sample of adequate size was obtained, involving approximately 100 students or more. Nearly all of the data were gathered during the 1959-60 school year from the records of teen-age Indian and non-Indian students in grades five through twelve.

A COMPARISON OF INDIAN AND NON-INDIAN I.Q. SCORES

In the spring of 1960, a battery of Lorge-Thorndike Intelligence Tests was given to the pupils in all grade levels at the Ft. Thomas Schools. An analysis of these results was made by Louis C. Bernardoni and his staff at the Department of Public Instruction, Division of Indian Education of the State of Arizona. The following is a summary of the major points of Bernardoni's findings.

The Lorge-Thorndike Intelligence Tests have been standardized for communities of varying socio-economic levels, and are adaptable to conditions where low socio-economic status has prevailed throughout the background of the subjects, a factor which made these tests seem to be favorably suited to most of the students at Ft. Thomas. Since the tests yielded both a verbal and non-verbal I.Q., it was possible to see if any differences existed between these separate performance categories that might help in evaluating the abilities of Apache students in both verbal and non-verbal tasks.

The students—both Indian and non-Indian—were grouped by grades 1-3, 4-6, and 7-12, in accordance with the design of the test. If it can be assumed that all of the students understood the instructions and were properly motivated in their performance, then we can regard the following aspects of the data with some validity. For the purposes of this study, the chief concern will be with the results from grades 4 through 12 only.

Table 1. Mean I.Q. Scores: Grades 4-6*

		INDIAN Total 47			NON-INDIAN Total 34	
Grade	N.	Verbal I.Q.	Non-Verbal I.Q.	N.	Verbal I.Q.	Non-Verbal I.Q.
4	14	74.57	73.35	13	98.00	94.31
5	16	70.31	82.69	9	104.44	104.66
6	17	77.12	92.65	12	96.00	103.66
Mean		74.06	83.62		99.00	100.35

Table 2. Mean I.Q. Scores: Grades 7-12*

		INDIAN Total 51			NON-INDIAN Total 53	
Grade	N.	Verbal I.Q.	Non-Verbal I.Q.	N.	Verbal I.Q.	Non-Verbal I.Q.
7	15	76.60	89.67	12	95.42	102.58
8	10	72.60	90.80	10	103.80	106.60
9	11	78.55	87.73	12	90.75	92.92
10	7	82.57	93.43	5	91.20	93.20
11	4	72.25	88.25	8	96.88	101.25
12	4	71.75	79.75	6	95.00	106.50
Mean		76.33	89.10		95.72	100.51

As can be seen from the mean I.Q. scores above, the non-Apache students tended to score somewhat near the national norms on the verbal tests and slightly above these norms on the non-verbal tests. The Apache students, however, tended to score below the national norms on both tests, to levels approximately 25 points lower on the verbal sections and 10-15 points lower on the non-verbal sections. The differences between the verbal and non-verbal I.Q.'s for Apaches were found to be statistically significant, an indication to some degree of the verbal handicap experienced by these students in school. (The assumption here is that a "slow learner" would have made similar low scores on both sections of the test.)

The Lorge-Thorndike Intelligence Tests also yielded a mean grade equivalent score that could be used in comparison with actual grade placement. In accordance with expectations, the Apache grade equivalent scores were far more erratic and considerably lower than the non-Apache scores. Non-verbal

---

*The National Standard mean I.Q. is 100.

grade equivalent scores were, on the whole, higher than the verbal scores for both Indians and non-Indians.

Table 3. Mean Grade Equivalent

Grade	Indian		Non-Indian	
	Verbal	Non-Verbal	Verbal	Non-Verbal
7	4.35	6.20	6.78	8.05
8	4.26	7.00	9.10	9.39
9	5.84	7.07	7.81	7.69
10	7.43	9.20	7.68	8.60
11	7.25	8.45	9.46	9.75
12	5.55	6.10	10.41	11.52

The results of Bernardoni's findings brought him to the following conclusions:

1) While the Lorge-Thorndike does not seem to be fair for these Apache students in that they (the students) do not score near the national norms, it may differentiate students with a language handicap from slow learners. It also seems to differentiate between verbal and non-verbal abilities for this bicultural, bilingual group.

2) There is a significant difference between Indian and non-Indian scores on this test, with Indian students scoring approximately 25 points lower on the verbal tests and 10 to 15 points lower on the non-verbal tests than non-Indian students. The difference between the verbal and non-verbal I.Q. scores for Indian students is also significant.

3) The Indian students tend to be about one year older than their classmates, and to average one letter grade lower in marks assigned by teachers..

4) The Lorge-Thorndike does not seem to predict academic achievement as measured by teachers' marks for Indian students.

5) This test should be evaluated further, using achievement tests, ratings of student intelligence, ratings of acculturation, parental interest in schools, etc. to gain a better perspective of this test (Bernardoni 1960:11).

From Bernardoni's analysis, it is evident that teen-age Apache students were not academically on a par with the standards of the grades in which they were enrolled. The experiment also pointed out the inadequacies of some psychological tests like the Lorge-Thorndike series in measuring the inherent capabilities of the Apache students. The best they can do, it seems, is to point out the handicaps of those whose cultural backgrounds differ from the Anglo norms upon which these tests are based.

A COMPARISON OF INDIAN AND NON-INDIAN SCHOLASTIC ACHIEVEMENT

The following comparative analysis of Indian and non-Indian scholastic achievement records was based on the data gathered in 1959-60 at the Ft. Thomas Public Schools for grades 5 through 12. The Ft. Thomas district was chosen in favor of Globe, primarily for two reasons: a) It had a total student enrollment of manageable size (less than 300), and b) the non-Indian students from the district had a somewhat rural, agricultural background, more like that of the Apache students. Globe was much more of an urban, mining and commercial area.

The school curriculum at Ft. Thomas was broken down into four major areas of study to help simplify the analysis:

I. The Language Arts—spelling, reading, phonics, literature, and English

II. The Historic & Geographic Arts—American and world history, geography, American government

III. Science and Mathematics—all science and math courses

IV. Manual and Vocational Arts—vocational agriculture, business and typing, home economics, and industrial arts

Grades were based on the following numerical scale:

1—excellent

2—good

3—average

4—below average

5—failure

In the Language Arts, Apache teen-age students fell below the 3.0 scholastic norm in all of the grades covered except the twelfth. Here they did manage to maintain a 3.0 in English. The non-Indians, on the other hand, maintained averages well above the 3.0 level in every class except one. The differences between Indian and non-Indian averages ranged from 0.1 to 1.8 grade points.

In Historic and Geographic Arts Apache students consistently remained at least 1.0 grade-points below their non-Indian peers in all classes. In Science and Mathematics the picture was the same, the Apache pupils averaging slightly less than 3.5 and the non-Indians slightly better than 2.5.

Scholastic differences became somewhat mixed in Manual and Vocational Arts. There is no doubt, however, that the Apache grades were improved. In industrial arts (classes 7-12) Apache grade averages came close to the 2.5 level, about one-half a grade-point below the non-Indians. In vocational agriculture (classes 9-12) Apache ninth graders did much poorer than their non-Indian peers—Apaches 3.4, non-Indians 1.3—but at the twelfth grade level both were close to a 2.5. In business and typing (classes 9-12) Apache ninth and tenth graders did approximately one-half a grade-point better than the non-Indian pupils; but in the eleventh and twelfth grades, a sudden reverse in this trend once more put them far apart, with Apaches at the 3.5 level, 1.5 grade-points below the non-Indians. Home economics, on the other hand (classes 9-12), provided the Apache pupils with their best grades in Manual and Vocational Arts, keeping them well above a 2.3. The non-Indian home economics students also did very well by maintaining a composite average of 1.5.

This brief analysis of comparative grade-point averages in relation to subject areas shows that the Apache students at Ft. Thomas achieved decidedly poorer grades in the more solid or academic subjects than did their non-Indian classmates. While a marked improvement was seen in Manual and Vocational Arts for the Apaches, these subjects have little importance in preparation for college admission requirements, a desired goal expressed by Apache leaders (Wesley 1961:4).

A summary of grade-point averages, lumping together all of the subject areas for Indian and non-Indian groups at each class level from grades five through twelve, points out the discrepancies between both groups even more vividly.

Table 4. Ft. Thomas Public Schools, 1959-1960

Grade Levels	Indians	Non-Indians	Difference
5	3.16	1.75	1.41
6	2.81	2.11	0.70
7	3.65	2.45	1.20
8	3.28	1.97	1.31
9	3.19	2.21	0.98
10	3.07	3.10	0.03*
11	3.27	2.17	1.10
12	2.69	2.06	0.63

*The combination of an advanced Apache group and a retarded non-Indian group created this exceptional reversal.

At Globe a similar summary grade-point analysis was made for the much larger Indian and non-Indian student groups at the elementary, junior high, and high school levels. The results added further evidence to the discrepancy between Apache and non-Indian scholastic achievement.

Table 5. Globe Public Schools, 1959-1960

Grade Levels	Indians	Non-Indians	Difference
5	4.03	2.52	1.51
6	3.49	2.81	0.68
7	3.88	3.07	0.81
8	3.99	3.16	0.83
9	3.72	2.98	0.74
10	3.71	3.07	0.64
11	*	3.03	*
12	3.68	2.61	1.07

*There were no Apaches in the eleventh grade at Globe High School in 1959-60.

Grade-point averages for teen-age Apache students in the federal and mission boarding schools tended to be somewhat higher than for those students attending the integrated public schools. This was believed to be in part the result of the absence of non-Indian competition in the boarding schools. In the off-reservation, integrated public schools there were many non-Indian low-achievers, but the high-achievers among the non-Indian group were very often the classroom pace-setters, offering stiff competition to low-achievers and Indians alike.

APACHE ACADEMIC RETARDATION AS INDICATED BY THE AGE-GRADE LAG

Along with standard I.Q. and achievement tests and grade-point averages, a third measure of academic achievement is the age-grade relationship: that is, the student's age in relation to the proper age for his grade level.

In most public schools and under normal circumstances, students are expected to begin at a standard age and thereafter progress from year to year at the normal rate of advancement. Thus each grade level maintains a standard age level, and the work is geared to match the anticipated intellectual level of the pupils at that age and phase of maturity. In the state of Arizona, for example, children are expected to begin the first grade at the age of 6 years. At the normal rate of advancement, then, they should finish the eighth grade by age 14 or 15 and the twelfth grade by age 17 or 18, depending upon the month in which they were born.

In the federal day schools at San Carlos and Bylas, as stated earlier, the Apache students in 1960 were compelled to begin the first grade at age 7, automatically placing them at least one year behind the standard age-grade level for public school students. With normal advancement, Apache students could not therefore be expected to finish the twelfth grade before ages 18 or 19. This standard age discrepancy between Indians and non-Indians does not complicate the analysis except for the fact that a double set of data must be described, in line with either the "Apache norm" or the "Anglo norm."

The degree of over-age Apache students at grade levels 5 through 12 will be discussed as the "age-grade lag," a measure of academic retardation. The tables below summarize the data gathered in 1959-60 from the Globe, Ft. Thomas, and Phoenix Indian School records. The figures are presented in the form of percentages of over-aged Apaches for each grade level in relation to Apache or Anglo norms (brackets).

As can be seen from the above three charts, there was a sizable age-grade lag among teen-age Apache students. At Globe, for example, approximately 47% were over-aged according to Apache norms. At Ft. Thomas, the number went up to 54%, while at three federal boarding schools, including

Table 6. Globe Public Schools

Grade Levels	5	6	7	8	9	10	11	12
% of over-aged Apaches according to "Apache norm"	42.7 (11)	24.7 (12)	29.7 (13)	46.2 (14)	51.2 (15)	33.2 (16)	* (17)	100.0 (18)
% of over-aged Apaches according to "Anglo norm"	87.3 (10)	89.1 (11)	84.2 (12)	82.7 (13)	100.0 (14)	100.0 (15)	* (16)	100.0 (17)

Table 7. Ft. Thomas Public Schools

Grade Levels	5	6	7	8	9	10	11	12
% of over-aged Apaches according to "Apache norm"	50.7 (11)	73.3 (12)	37.5 (13)	41.6 (14)	73.4 (15)	50.0 (16)	62.5 (17)	40.0 (18)
% of over-aged Apaches according to "Anglo norm"	84.0 (10)	93.3 (11)	100.0 (12)	83.3 (13)	80.1 (14)	80.0 (15)	100.0 (16)	100.0 (17)

Table 8. Phoenix Indian School

Grade Levels	5	6	7	8	9	10	11	12
% of over-aged Apaches according to "Apache norm"	63.5 (11)	87.5 (12)	78.5 (13)	55.5 (14)	62.9 (15)	40.0 (16)	60.0 (17)	55.5 (18)
% of over-aged Apaches according to "Anglo norm"	91.0 (10)	100.0 (11)	92.9 (12)	96.3 (13)	96.3 (14)	100.0 (15)	90.0 (16)	77.8 (17)

*No Apaches in grade 11 at Globe during 1959-60.

Phoenix Indian School, over 63% of the enrolled Apaches were older than expected for their particular grade levels.

A closer look at the data showed that within many of the classes or grade levels, the spread of age differences was considerable. In the Globe schools, for example, within grades 5, 6, 7, and 8, the age spread was as great as 6, 7, 6, and 5 years, respectively. There were 16-year-old pupils attending classes with 9-year-olds, 17-year-old pupils in classes with 11-year-olds, and so forth.

Such tremendous age differences between Apache students of the same grade level presented many problems not only for the teacher, but for the students as well. Differences in physical maturity sometimes caused conflicts between students during play periods or sports activities. A student 4 or 5 years older than the norm found little to interest him in class materials that were geared for students at a much younger stage of emotional and motivational development. Occasionally such older Apache students in the public schools would lose interest in school, feel embarrassed at being in class with "younger kids," and drop out of their own accord. If possible, they were picked up again and sent off to boarding school where there were many students like them from other tribes, of the same age and grade.

In addition to all of these problems, a matter of simple practicality remained unanswered: How much longer can one keep in school Apache children who are already 15, 16, and 17 years old, and have not yet reached the eighth grade? At least one of the public schools was found to have an answer to this question, and it shall be discussed at this time as a separate measure of Apache academic achievement in school.

"SOCIAL PROMOTIONS" FOR OVER-AGE APACHE STUDENTS

When the survey of grade-point averages for Apaches in the public schools was being made, special attention was paid to the transition years, grades 5 and 6. This was the point where many Apaches experienced their first taste of integration in the classes with non-Indians. This was also the point where many experienced for the first time schooling away from home, in an atmosphere where Indians were in the minority and where teachers and school policies were not oriented towards Indians as in the reservation federal day schools or mission schools.

As mentioned earlier, some Apache students admitted considerable difficulty when trying to adjust to new experiences during those transition years. A few remarked it was the first time they had ever had homework! Such indications tended to support the views of some Apache leaders that the on-reservation schools were not adequately preparing Apaches for the demands of the off-reservation public schools (Wesley 1961:4).

In consideration of these factors, then, was there a noticeable lag in the academic achievement of Apache students during this transitional period? Grade-point summaries showed that the non-Indian fifth and sixth graders had exceptionally high averages at both Globe and Ft. Thomas public schools. The Apache students, however, did not do so well. In the fifth grade, for example, Apaches received grade-point averages that were approximately 1.5 points lower than those of their non-

Indian classmates. In the sixth grade this margin was somewhat reduced.

Additional information from the records at East Globe Elementary School made this writer wonder if the grade-point averages were telling the whole story. Alongside some of the students' grades was found the notation: "social promotion." When asked to clarify the interpretation of this term, the school principal stated:

> In our school a teacher will give a student a social promotion to the next grade if he has failed to pass the academic requirements for his present grade, but has reached an age where retention is no longer beneficial to the student or his classmates.
>
> (from a personal conversation with principal)

At the end of the 1959-60 school year, the records showed that no less than 44.4% of the Apache fifth graders at East Globe Elementary were socially promoted to grade 6, and 60.0% of the Apache sixth graders were socially promoted to grade 7. In line with the quotation above, it can be said that over 50% of the Apache pupils in those classes were over-age and unable to fulfill the required work for their respective grades.

One wonders how many of these social promotions occurred unrecorded in other grades and schools. One point, however, seems certain: Students promoted primarily on the basis of age rather than academic achievement must have found the following year's demands even more frustrating to cope with. Without substantial remedial assistance, these cumulative deficiencies would grow from year to year to cause Apaches to fall farther behind academically and farther away from any hopes of graduation.

THE DROP-OUT RATE AMONG APACHE TEEN-AGERS

Perhaps one of the most difficult things for which to obtain accurate data was the actual drop-out rate for Apache teen-agers. First of all, when did a student become a drop-out? Considered on the basis of withdrawal only, there were hundreds of Apache drop-outs, for there was never an end to unauthorized mid-year withdrawals. Immediate follow-ups of such withdrawals by local reservation authorities were undoubtedly responsible for preventing many actual drop-out cases among Apache teen-agers, since a large portion were eventually transferred to other schools (see pp. 42-43).

A student was generally considered a true drop-out after every effort to return him to school had failed and he remained out of school for at least a year. Such students were usually near or past the legal age of 18, when the tribal compulsory education laws no longer applied. The methods of keeping drop-out records on the reservation were not very accurate, however, and it was difficult to tell each year what the actual drop-out rate was. Any individual case might remain on the list for several years until he was forgotten.

From the records maintained by the staff of this project, some 86 Apaches were identified as drop-outs in 1959-60, but less than half that number had actually withdrawn from school in that same year. Their reasons for withdrawal from school were many, some of which have already been touched upon: lack of family support, discouragement about school, marriage, a family need at home, illness, unwed and with child, etc. Of the 86 drop-outs, 50 were girls and 36 were boys. Most of the girls had gotten married. Very few of the boys had succeeded in finding even part-time work. Usually they roamed about their home communities in groups socializing and drinking and occasionally getting into trouble.

It was very evident to this writer, however, that the actual drop-out rate should have been higher, considering the low academic achievement of some Apaches in school. In spite of the efforts of school administrators and tribal officials, some students had mentally and emotionally withdrawn from the existing efforts to educate them, even though they were physically in attendance at school (see page 47).

POST-HIGH SCHOOL ENROLLMENT OF APACHES IN COLLEGES AND TRAINING SCHOOLS

In 1961, Clarence Wesley (1961:4), Chairman of the San Carlos Apache Tribe, reported that: "In recent years no Indian from the San Carlos Apache reservation has graduated from college, though several have started." While this statement is not entirely correct (see page 23) it does bespeak a situation that has serious consequences for the entire tribe. There are very few college trained or skilled Apaches available to manage tribal affairs. The extremely small minority of Apache high school graduates entering college over the past decade have produced virtually no graduates outside of a mission school teacher or two and possibly a business college graduate. The numbers in vocational schools have been larger, but many graduates were unable to return to the reservation to put their training to use because of the lack of local employment opportunities. In a word, there have been relatively few Apaches trained beyond high school to meet the professional needs of the reservation; and of the few trained, it seems only a small minority were able to apply their skills to the needs of their people.

Presented below are the figures from the BIA San Carlos Agency annual school census reports for the period 1949-1961.

Table 9. San Carlos Apaches Enrolled in Colleges and Vocational Schools, 1949-1961

School Year	Enrollment in College	Enrollment in Vocational Schools
1949-50	2	24
1950-51	5	20
1951-52	1	10
1952-53	2	1
1953-54	11	6
1954-55	10	3
1955-56	14	5
1956-57	12	12
1957-58	4	19
1958-59	6	16
1959-60	7	16
1960-61	5	11

A break-down of these figures was obtained for the 1959-60 school year, showing that in the vocational schools 9 were taking training in welding, 3 were learning to be barbers, 3 were enrolled in nursing programs, and one was in a hospital studying x-ray technology. Of the 7 in college for that year, 4 were training to be office clerks, one was studying business administration, one was learning animal husbandry, and one was preparing for elementary teaching.

Considering that the main economic resources on the San Carlos Reservation were cattle, lumber, and subsistence farming, there would not have been much use for the talents of 9 welders and 3 barbers. The rest could have fitted into the economy at the time, but possibly as much as half of the total group would have had to look for employment elsewhere in order to apply their acquired trades. On the other hand, very little was being done to meet the growing demands of an expanding reservation community which would require teachers, business managers, health and welfare personnel, lawyers and judges, carpenters and plumbers, mechanics, electricians, agricultural specialists, engineers, and other professionally trained personnel. Such positions existed on the San Carlos Reservation, but for the most part were held by non-Apache personnel.

Looking towards a brighter future, the tribal council sought to develop new sources of economic gain and employment: tourism, light industry, better housing, roads, and communications; but in turning to their own manpower resources, there were very few with adequate training who could take on such responsibilities. Apparently matters had not substantially improved by 1964, if the confidential *Survey of the San Carlos Reservation* (Arizona Commission of Indian Affairs 1964b) is accurate. In February of that year only five Apaches were reported to be in college, and another five in vocational schools. March, 1964, employment figures were no less discouraging. Full-time positions held by Apaches working on the reservation numbered only 80:

    40 for the tribal council and tribal enterprises
    20 for the Bureau of Indian Affairs
    15 for other state or federal agencies
     5 in agriculture
            (Arizona Commission of Indian Affairs 1964b)

The facts and figures presented thus far in this chapter might lead one to ask a number of questions. In what way did cultural differences, home and community conditions, and school policies contribute to the failures of Apache teen-agers in school? To what extent did personal motivation become involved with academic achievement for young Apaches? Was school the only problem area for these students? Could Apache parents have helped to avoid some of these problems?

Some of the answers to these questions have already been mentioned, but the major burden of probing into the factors surrounding these questions and answers, will be left up to Chapter 4.

Factors Affecting the Education of Apache Youth

THE DISCUSSION OF FACTORS contributing to the academic and personal problems of Apache teen-agers will be divided into three main parts: 1) problems stemming from the community, 2) problems stemming from the family, and 3) problems stemming from the education program. Before getting into the first of these topics, however, a sample of case histories illustrating some of the more significant problems and their underlying causes, as described by the data presented in the last chapter will be reviewed. Interviews and personal records from school and agency files were used to compile more than 30 detailed case histories, from which the four presented here were selected.

CASE HISTORY NO. 1: "DANNY"*

Danny was born in 1944, the illegitimate son of his unwed Apache mother and Anglo father. He never saw his father, but he did vaguely remember the man his mother married shortly after Danny was born. He was a Navajo. When his mother went off to live with her Navajo husband, Danny was left behind at San Carlos to be raised by his maternal grandparents. Once in a great while Danny's grandparents were visited by his mother and her husband, but he did not care for either of them and was glad they had left him at San Carlos. Although his grandparents were old and nearly blind, they showed their love for him; and even as a little boy, he felt responsible in caring for them.

The home that Danny shared with his grandparents was

---

*All names presented in the four case histories below are fictitious.

a small wooden frame house with a single room 12' x 14' located on a barren plot of ground at Gilson Wash. There was no gas or electricity, and water came from an outdoor tap. Heating and cooking was done on a wood stove. They had no car, and getting around to the store, the church, and the hospital took many hours of walking. Out of the small pension Danny's grandfather received, they purchased the barest essentials. Sometimes when this was not enough the local welfare agent helped them out.

Danny attended a variety of schools before entering the school program at Globe. He attended the local mission school, the government school at San Carlos, and for brief periods two public schools. His attendance was good, according to the records, and his teachers spoke highly of him. They said he was "quick to learn," "speaks English well and like[d] numbers," and that he was a "top student in class" when he was in the sixth grade at San Carlos. But when Danny entered the seventh grade in Globe the record of his achievements fell.

At Globe Junior High Danny did so poorly the first year that he was conditionally promoted to the eighth grade. In the eighth grade his marks improved slightly, but still he got mostly 4's. Danny explained his problem basically in these terms:

1) When he left the reservation Indian school and entered the integrated public school, he realized he was far behind the non-Indians in his class. It took him a great deal of effort to catch up and to try and keep up with the others.

2) There was no encouragement to study at home. There was, in fact, no place to study. Thus he seldom studied at home. His grandparents did not compel him to study; when his chores around the house were done, he simply went off to "goof around with the other kids."

Throughout, Danny's attendance was excellent. His I.Q. and achievement test scores were approximately average, which was higher than other Apaches. In 1960, however, his mother returned to the little house at Gilson Wash with a Pima man, her husband having died earlier of TB. One night she received an almost fatal beating from this man, the result of excessive mutual drinking, and was rushed to the hospital. The Pima man was banished from the Apache reservation by tribal authorities.

By now Danny had made friends with his high school music teacher, Mr. Donald, who had befriended the boy on numerous occasions. When the crisis at Danny's home occurred, it upset the boy greatly, and the local authorities agreed to permit Danny to live with the Donald family in Globe. Danny worried about his grandparents, but the Donalds took him to visit them often. He also visited his mother at the hospital, but this he soon stopped. Mr. Donald said it depressed Danny greatly each time.

Danny's grades finally began to show signs of improvement. A simply inquiry brought a rather enthusiastic response: "Man, you should see what I have now," he said. "I've got my own room, my own desk, my own lamp, and everything! We even have a set of encyclopedias in the house, and I use it all the time. Sometimes when I don't want to study they (the Donalds) make me study. They *push* me into it!" Danny's tone evinced his approval.

Danny liked the attention the Donalds were showing him. "Whenever I have a problem, I just go to [Mr. Donald] and he helps me." He never had a father or maternal uncle to turn to before. Other Apaches shunned him because he was a "half-breed" and not one of them. It hurt him at first, but he did not seem to resent this as much as one might have expected. In fact, he felt sorry for the other Apache children. They seldom discussed their personal lives with their parents, he said, and their parents did not inquire. School matters were almost never mentioned unless a child was sick. "The parents aren't interested in their children," he rationalized. "They don't care what their kids do. They tell them, 'You can go out and work as a cowboy, it doesn't matter.' They don't care if their kids do well in school or not."

It was not long before the Donalds adopted Danny. He went less often to the reservation and worked in Globe during the summers. He even started dating an Anglo girl, after the

Donalds had pacified her parents. Donald felt that adult Anglos were far more prejudiced than their children. Apache students resented Danny's behavior and rejected his friendship, but he did not seem to care any more.

CASE HISTORY NO. 2: "BERT"

Bert was the oldest boy and fourth in a line of eleven children. His father was the son of an early Apache scout who, while in the service of Captain Crawford during the late 1800's, aided in the capture of Geronimo, and was later assigned to guard the fallen leader in his eastern prison camp in Oklahoma. In 1960 the family lived in pleasant surroundings at Seven-Mile Wash, in a better-than-average three-room frame house, as well as two additional houses. The grounds were well kept, and the family enjoyed electricity, running water, and the use of radios, a washing machine, and two pick-up trucks. Bert's father was a steady, reliable worker, holding a rather prominent position in community health services. He had the equivalent of an eighth-grade education, but was considered by his employers to have learned far more through his own personal efforts since the time of his school training.

Bert's parents were strongly education-oriented. He and his brothers and sisters all had excellent attendance records throughout their school careers. Nearly all had average or better than average achievement records, and one of Bert's older sisters even went on to junior college, but she found it quite difficult. Their home life was exceptionally stable and harmonious in spite of the size of the family—a result of the father's firm discipline and strong sense of family responsibility.

Bert stayed in Indian schools until he was in the seventh grade. Then he started attending school at Globe. He said that the transition for him was very hard. For the first time he had to do homework, and his parents provided a place for him to study at home. His marks were very poor that year and his attendance was far below his average for the other years. The non-Indians, he said, were hard to compete with and he found English difficult.

Bert was promoted to the eighth grade, and when his

work did not improve, he was granted a "social promotion" to grade 9. He took remedial English his freshman year in high school but failed it along with general math, business, and world geography. He was held back at the end of the year, and after taking over some of these courses, was allowed to become a sophomore in 1960. His grades remained poor and it was obvious from the interviews that he was discouraged. His father, in fact, had expressed deep concern about the boy's future. He blamed Bert's troubles on a newly acquired interest in girls, and he made formidable efforts at breaking up all possible romances, convinced that only firm discipline would get the boy's mind back on his education, "where it should be." But all of Bert's problems were not female, and the following incident, revealed at an interview, illustrates a rather frequent occurrence among Apache students in school.

During an interview Bert announced one day that he was going to fail biology. The class had been assigned a semester project, and Bert had chosen to write a 7,500 word paper on radiation biology. He picked this topic because it had sounded interesting to him, but when he learned how complex a subject it was, he knew he could not handle it. Two weeks later he asked to have his topic changed, but the instructor refused. Now, the day before it was due, Bert had not written a single word.

A subsequent inquiry revealed that had Bert made an attempt at completing his project, he might have passed the course, but he had not discussed this possibility at the time with his instructor. He had also failed to approach the Indian student counselor with his problem and, in fact, appeared to be ignorant of the man's function in the school program. Bert had not mentioned a word of his dilemma to his parents.

When asked if he ever confided in others concerning his own personal matters, Bert replied that he sometimes wanted to talk to someone about such things very much, but he knew of no one in whom he could confide. He did not talk to his parents because he was certain they would not understand. His good pal, Harry, was a quiet fellow and they seldom talked about personal matters; so Bert kept most things to himself. If a guy went around with a girl, he said, most (Apache) people said they should get married. It was hard to go dating like the white boys and Mexicans. There was really no one a guy could confide in, and he just did not "have the guts" to ask people for help.

When told that he would probably have to take biology over again, Bert replied smiling, "Oh, I don't mind. It's one of my favorite subjects." Later he added, "I'm gonna be 18 this August. Maybe I'll just quit an' stay around home like the other guys."

CASE HISTORY NO. 3: "LYDIA"

Lydia lived in Bylas, and in 1960 attended the seventh grade class at Ft. Thomas. Her father had been a part-time laborer all his life, except when he was an Army scout in 1928. Both her father and her mother had been previously married and had large families.

According to the local welfare worker, Lydia's parents had never really maintained a stable home for their children. The family income had for years been sporadic and seldom sufficient to meet the barest needs. They were often dependent on welfare and assistance from relatives, and the children had to be "farmed-out" whenever one or both parents were jailed for drunkenness. When sober they talked about education, but they seemed to prefer to send their children off to boarding school where others could take care of the task. Nearly all of Lydia's older sisters were married now, but the rest of her siblings were still in school as she was, making failing grades and showing poor attendance. Their life together as a family was to "live and shift" (social worker) from one day to the next.

In 1960 Lydia had to borrow clothes in order to go to school. With no home to go to each night, she would "run around," as Apaches would say, going from house to house with friends—some of whom were in the same plight as she— and with the groups of boys who dared to disobey the curfew. Sometimes Lydia would stay with an older sister, but her sister's husband was out of work most of the time, and occasionally he spent some time in jail. She claimed she saw little of her parents.

Lydia said she liked school but found it very hard. Her father and her sister wanted her to stay in school. She said she liked her father because he bought her clothes now and then, but her mother wanted her to quit school because she was ashamed of what people were saying about Lydia's nighttime habits. Lydia did not like her mother and tried to ignore what she said. She said her mother never did anything for her. Lydia preferred to be with her two girl friends most of the time, even though they teased her when the other Apaches did. But they were the only two girls she could talk to, she said.

Lydia was two years over the Apache age norm for her grade. Her marks were mostly failures, and her teachers complained that she was a "complete blank" in class, never responding to anything they said or tried to do. She seldom spoke to Anglos and stayed mostly with other Indian students. She was accused by her teachers of not caring about school and having no pride in her appearance. She was known to drink whenever she could obtain liquor, and sometimes after drinking too much she would go to the homes of friends for food and shelter.

As might be expected, Lydia had very little to say about her own future. She said if she could not stay in school, she would simply "stay at home"—wherever that might be. She admitted, though, that there was nothing for her to do at home. Probing deeper than this only provoked a sad and silent response, a response that answered no questions, but succeeded nearly always in curtailing any further discussion.

CASE HISTORY NO. 4: "JED"

Jed was the third oldest boy out of nine children. His father was a high school graduate and a prominent tribal leader from Bylas, active in politics, law, and church functions. His mother was a quiet, unassuming woman, devoted to her family. They had a larger than average home of brick construction with most household conveniences. In recent years up to 1960 the family enjoyed a steady income and an exceptional degree of harmonious stability, in spite of the father's occasional political battles.

Jed's academic achievement over the years was exceptional. In the seventh grade at Ft. Thomas his lowest grade was a 3— (1 is excellent) in geography. In the eighth grade his marks were mostly 1's and 2's. His lowest mark in the ninth grade was a 3+ in history. In the tenth grade at Ft. Thomas he had nearly a 1 average in all of his "solid" courses. His lowest grade in the eleventh grade was a 2. Jed managed a straight 1.0 grade-point average in English since the eighth grade! His total attendance record was excellent. Among Indians and non-Indians, Jed was considered by his teachers to be an outstanding student, both intelligent and very diligent.

Jed was aware of his accomplishments and did not hesitate to discuss them with the author, although he was never boastful. He attributed his success to plain hard work. He said he studied in school and at home every day, even though some of the other Apache students chided him for it. He blamed the failures of many Apaches in school on the fact that they gave up too easily when in competition with non-Indians. Jed seemed convinced that many Apaches could do as well as he if only they would put aside their defeatist attitude and work harder at their studies.

This was one reason why Jed did not pal around with other Apache boys. He felt that their interests differed from his. They only wanted to "fool around" and had no interest in school or the future. They had, as he put it, "nothing to offer" him. Jed's best pal was a scholarly Mexican boy from whom he learned Spanish and better English. In spite of the resentment expressed by his Apache peers, Jed remarked confidently, "I can handle myself. I'm not afraid of what they say."

Others were also aware of Jed's exceptional standards, and it was usually easy for him to find a job during vacation periods. His relations with his family seemed good, although he preferred to confide more in an older sister or his mother than with his father. The only thing he would say about his father was to admit that he gave Jed money when needed.

When Jed announced to his parents his desire to become a lawyer, he was disappointed that his father, at least, had no comment to make and no encouragement to offer. What, then, did motivate Jed to work so hard at his studies?

Jed unhesitatingly replied that he was in heated competition with the non-Indian students in his school. They were out to beat him, he asserted, but he was not going to let them get ahead of him. He realized how much hard work had accomplished, and he was determined to stay on the top of the heap. Much of the time during each interview was spent discussing his plans for college and the many opportunities available for scholarships.

The above case histories represent a very small sample of the many, many similar cases encountered by the author and his research team during the two and one-half year period of the study. The incidents and views described are merely intended to illustrate some of the more typical findings revealed through hundreds of personal interviews with parents, teachers, community service officers, and students, in order that the reader might visualize more clearly the relationship between the problems of Apache teen-agers in school and those experienced at home on the reservation.

"Danny" and "Lydia" represent those Apache youngsters with poor home and family backgrounds—a lack of parental love (although Danny at least had his grandparents) and responsible care, economic instability, and moral depravity where parental guidance and discipline should have prevailed. But Danny's outlook and academic achievement did not parallel Lydia's.

For one thing, Danny was a boy and in Apache society he could move about more freely than Lydia, with less to fear from public criticism. "Runnin' around at night" was a criticism far less consequential for boys than for Apache girls. Lydia was socially "branded" as a bad girl, and even though people might admit that she was not entirely to blame for her situation, mothers of other boys and girls had already "blackballed" her as an undesirable companion for their own children. Her chances of eventually marrying into a good local family were seriously limited, if not altogether lost. Apache boys, on the other hand, involved in the same activities when youths, would sooner or later be pardoned because of the prevailing attitude among Apaches that "boys will be boys."*

Although Danny spoke of himself as an Apache, he realized that his half-white heritage (his physical appearance was predominantly Caucasian) would always be a barrier to his complete acceptance by Apaches. This enabled him to rationalize more easily any rejection that he experienced, for he could not blame himself for the folly of his parents. The fact that Anglos—his adopted parents in particular—were willing to accept him gave him an opportunity to develop new interests, goals, and values. His new home, with its relatively luxurious surroundings and facilities, and more importantly, the abundance of close personal attention received from his new parents, gave Danny a new sense of personal worth and pride. It afforded him an opportunity to achieve success as defined by his Anglo parents, and in so doing, to please those for whom he now had a strong feeling of affection and responsibility.

Lydia was not so fortunate. There was really very little hope for her to regain all that she had lost as long as she remained among her people. This is not to say that being adopted into an Anglo family like Danny would be the best solution for all such teen-agers, but rather that as long as Lydia remained in Bylas, she would always have the stigma of her wayward youth, a serious obstacle for her or any Apache girl in her predicament. As it was, she had little in life to look forward to and consequently less cause to strive for improve-

---

*A more striking example of this phenomenon occurred when a teen-age Apache girl was one night raped by a half dozen Apache youths. The boys were later brought before the local tribal magistrate on charges initiated by the girl's parents. But the boys' families brought counter-charges against the girl. The hearing proved that even though the girl willingly got into the boys' car "to go for a ride," she was forcibly molested by the older boys who overpowered her. The boys' parents, however, charged that she was a "bad girl" for being out at night and agreeing to go with the boys. The hearing ended with the judge sentencing the girl to a term in jail and criticizing her for being an evil influence in the community. The boys were released into the custody of their parents and told not to associate with such bad girls (Parmee 1959-1961a; 209-211).

ment, though under the circumstances improvement would have been exceedingly difficult. There were, regrettably, a great many Apache teen-age girls in Lydia's category.

Both "Jed" and "Bert" had stable home lives, with Apache fathers of notable community rank and personal achievement. There were also older brothers and sisters in both families who had attained comparatively good high school records and were now holding steady jobs. On the surface, at least, it appeared that both boys had equal opportunities for personal academic advancement, and yet their respective views towards the future and records of success were entirely different. Why?

Personality differences are clearly evident when comparing these two boys, although it is difficult to determine at this point whether the differences in personality contributed to the differences in achievement, or vice versa. Jed expressed personal confidence, strong motivation, and even aggressiveness, a rather atypical trait for Apache teen-agers in general. Bert, on the other hand, was rather timid in front of Anglos, showed very little self-confidence about his ability to improve in school, and had the more common Apache-student tendency to retreat from problems, rather than to attempt a partial success or to ask for aid.

Although Jed was not accepted by Anglos in the same manner as Danny was, his attitudes and achievements were clearly recognized by his teachers and non-Indian peers. He preferred this kind of recognition to recognition from other Apache boys, many of whom scorned his "White man's ways." Instead of retreating from competition, Jed regarded it as a means to obtain personal satisfaction. His closest friend, a Mexican boy, was his staunchest competitor.

Both Bert and Jed had since childhood been strongly encouraged by their families to "get a good education." For some reason, Bert had failed to respond to the opportunities afforded him by his family. Unfortunately, there was no psychological test of proven reliability available that could have been used to evaluate any differences in the potential intellectual aptitude of the two boys, for it would have been difficult to ascertain how much of the results was attributable to differences in individual English language abilities.

Bert acted discouraged, as if he had already "tossed in the towel" and resigned himself to whatever fate had in store for him. Jed, however, was definitely goal-oriented. He wanted to be a lawyer. Even more he perhaps wanted to prove to others that all Apaches were not "dumb" and "lazy," and that with persistent efforts, he could equal or even better his Anglo competitors in a world of their own design.

Factors Within the Community Environment

ECONOMIC PROBLEMS

Earlier in this report (see pp. 20-21) some effort was made to point out the serious unemployment problem existing on the San Carlos Apache Reservation. It is a problem that was carefully studied by the Stanford Research Institute in 1954 (Robison, et al.), that also prevailed on the reservation during the period of this study from 1959-61, and that still persists (Arizona Commission of Indian Affairs 1964b).

Such widespread Apache unemployment has come about as the result of a number of factors:

a) Full-scale development of the reservation economic resources has not been achieved. Enterprises such as mining and large-scale farming have died out, and timber harvesting has been extremely limited due to the inaccessibility of much of the forested areas (Robison et al. 1954: 129-131). Leasing contracts, and power and water problems have plagued efforts to attract light industry. Tourism is growing, but heavy investments are necessary to make good roads into the higher mountain areas, which are more suitable for camping, hunting, and fishing. Cattle-raising has been the tribe's chief industry, but even that has not been developed to its most lucrative limits:

> Thus it becomes evident that, through the years, traditional values have operated to prevent the San Carlos from becoming aware of a necessary shift in work habits, orientation to kin, and sociability if a successful cattle

enterprise is to develop. In place of sustained work and thrift, which alone can contribute capital for present and future needs, they retain a traditional work pattern based on periodic and irregular activity. Instead of stressing individual enterprise and responsibility for personal needs within a narrow family unit, they emphasize voluntary cooperation and the sharing of surplus within extended kin groups. And, when isolation on the range is essential to future benefits, they are prone to remain within comfortable range of neighbors and kin. San Carlos Apache values are in direct opposition to the demands of the market economy (Getty 1961-62: 185).

b) During the period of this study it was observed that individual commercial enterprises among Apaches were rather rare. Commercial enterprising throughout the reservation was dominated by tribal interests, managed by tribal employees, and directed by council authority. According to the 1964 San Carlos Survey only 40 to 45 Apaches were employed by the combined Tribal Council and Tribal Enterprise system (Arizona Commission of Indian Affairs (1964b). Individual commercial enterprises were usually discouraged by the dearth of individual capital resources, and the unavailability of loans for such purposes. Some tribal leaders admitted that the tribal enterprise system itself defeated potential individual enterprises by the very fact that it was such an overpowering competitor with strong political backing. This was in part a result of the fact that the tribal council budget came primarily from the income procured through tribal enterprises.

c) As has already been mentioned (see pp. 66-69), the lack of suitable occupational training among Apaches greatly reduced the number of possible job holders on the reservation, and non-Apaches had to be brought in to fulfill most skilled and technical positions.

d) Apaches, on the whole, were opposed to moving off the reservation to procure jobs. Efforts in the past to relocate Apaches never fully succeeded (Parmee 1961: 24-25) in spite of tribal efforts to encourage this program (Arizona Commission of Indian Affairs 1964b). Apaches preferred living in their own communities, regardless of the economic deprivations, to living isolated in distant non-Indian communities (Parmee 1959-1961a: 127-135).

Although there are no family economic surveys known to this author for the San Carlos Apaches, one can safely surmise from the data presented thus far that family poverty among these people was not uncommon. The effects of this upon the individual families and the lives of each family member will be discussed later; here the concern is the reservation community as a whole.

Many Apaches were in the position of supporting three governments out of their income taxes: federal, state, and tribal. A low income and a large family spared many from doling out funds to the first two governments, but since about 1960 all cattle sales were taxed 2½ % to help defray tribal council costs. Many Apaches opposed the passage of this bill, but at the time the council was desperately in need of additional funds.

In recent years the Apache tribal council continually struggled to keep its budget in the black. Caught between the desire to enact new programs for the improvement of reservation conditions and the threat of economic bankruptcy, the tribal council nearly every year found itself dependent upon alien sources for support of its programs. Federal agencies such as the BIA and U.S. Public Health Service spent millions on the San Carlos Reservation within the past decade to provide a multitude of community services: i.e., roads, welfare, range and agricultural improvement, education, hospital care, water and sanitation, disease control, etc. State welfare services also were at work on the reservation, and private charitable organizations each year lent their financial support to youth projects and individual needy families.

In the field of education the Apache tribe had for years been almost entirely dependent upon the BIA for financial aid and technical assistance. Consequently, Apaches had very little to say about the design and operation of their school programs. Requests by tribal leaders for improvements in the schools were continually held in abeyance by federal regulations, fiscal policies, and the opinions of BIA officials.* Even many of the basic goals of the program were of Anglo rather than Apache origin, and most decisions concerning operational or policy changes were entirely in the hands of the BIA.

Such conditions caused tribal leaders to appear impotent in the eyes of their people and they caused the people to harbor resentment towards the federal government, or Anglos in general, for what was felt to be social and political suppression (Parmee 1959-1961a: 241-245). Equally unfortunate was the fact that continued dependency of this sort produced apathy and ignorance among the Apache people, of the kind brought to light during the discussion of causes for absenteeism above (see pp. 47-50). Unable to think of the program as their own, many Apaches merely paid it a kind of lip-service, that was neither uncooperative nor affirmative. As a result of this attitude, attempts at community-school activities (PTA organizations and the like) often failed. The sole exception to this was the tribal education committee.

This tribally-appointed voluntary committee, whose functions have already been described on page 38, was, at the time of this study, a partial success. Taking its various functions point-by-point:

a) It provided educational loans for needy students, but the funds were very limited (a revolving fund of less than $6,000), and usually the committee had a very difficult time getting loans returned and keeping political influences from creeping into application approvals. The Committee also heard many complaints from parents against the school program, but seldom could facilitate any reciprocal action without the consent of the BIA.

b) Community projects such as sporting events, the local newspaper, summer camp programs, and scouting activities were usually sponsored by the tribal education committee, but its very limited funds, derived at the time solely from its own resources, hindered the committee from taking much more

---

*For example, pre-school classes for 5 year olds, more on-reservation day schools, language specialists, etc. (Wesley 1961: 4-7).

than a kind of diplomatic role in any of the larger projects.

c) The committee aided in the disbursement of private welfare funds to families with needy school children. Very often the degree of committee influence or popularity with the people was directly proportionate to the extent of its control over potential welfare resources.

d) The tribal education committee acted as a very important liason service between the common people and educational officialdom in the various separate school systems. It also provided—when funds or borrowed transportation permitted—many Apache parents with the opportunity to visit their children in distant schools. Occasionally Apache high school students were taken to visit a variety of colleges and training schools.

Some Apaches and Anglos laughed at this committee, pointing out its numerous weaknesses and informalities, but it was, in fact, at that time the most significant recent attempt on the part of Apaches to initiate some degree of constructive, active participation in a program of vital importance to their future social and economic progress.*

SOCIAL PROBLEMS

Unlike many rural American communities that thrive in an atmosphere of PTA's, church and social clubs, civic committees, and adult-sponsored youth activities, Apaches found it difficult to establish enough volunteer citizenship aid to meet growing community needs. Attempts by some to organize civic support in this manner failed numerous times during the period of this study.

In San Carlos, for example, unsuccessful attempts were made from time to time to organize a PTA group including both Anglo and Apache parents. Anglos blamed it on Apache parental apathy. Apaches said it was because Anglos dominated all of the meetings and that the group had no influence with the agencies operating the school program. The tribal education

---

*From a personal letter by the author to Marvin Mull, Chairman, San Carlos Apache Tribe, March 8, 1962.

committee, they said, at least had the ear of the council and was run by Apache leaders (Parmee 1959-1961a: 23-24).

In 1960, however, there were other tribally-appointed committees that did not function as effectively as the education committee, which met at least once every month and had year-round projects under way. A great deal depended upon the individual leadership of the committees, and although some of it was very weak, few Apaches were willing to openly criticize the councilmen who were in charge. The fact was, some Apaches did not understand this Anglo-American concept of civic and committee leadership, and for this reason hesitated to take active command of their assigned positions (Parmee 1959-1961a: 94-95).

Even among the few citizens' groups that did exist at San Carlos during the time of this study (i.e., women's hospital auxiliary, Boy Scouts, church parish clubs), cooperative activities seldom occurred and inter-group channels of communication were very weak or non-existent.

The management of law and order on the San Carlos Apache Reservation was a major responsibility of the tribal council. Each year it involved the largest council expenditure, which included the salaries of Apache judges, jailers, policemen and juvenile officers, plus all of their operational and vehicular expenses. From the many interviews with reservation officials, families, and tribal leaders, it was evident that alcoholism and its concurrent side-effects comprised one of the greatest law and order problems for the San Carlos Apaches (Parmee 1959-1961a: 36-38). As will be seen from the summary of court records below, juveniles (ages 10-17 years) as well as adults were affected.

In June of 1959, a survey of juvenile court records was made covering the period of June 1, 1958, through May 31, 1959. The following is a summary of these findings:

a) Out of more than 90% of all juveniles arrested, 26% were 16-year-olds, 25% were 17-year-olds, 25% were 15-year-olds, and 14% were 14-year-olds. The remaining 8% or so included age groups 10 through 13 years.

b) April, May, June, July, August, and December had the highest rate of arrests, averaging 27 cases per month.

c) The range of charges for arrest ran as follows:
—disorderly conduct, drunkenness,
   disobedience* 55%
—curfew violation 7%
—assault 6%
—carrying a concealed weapon............................ 6%
—theft 5%
—smoking, failure to go to school, running away
   from home, traffic violation, illicit cohabitation,
   vandalism, resisting arrest, escape from jail,
   and parole violation ....each less than 5%

d) Out of 180 recorded court decisions, 90 juveniles were given probation, 76 were given jail terms ranging from 10 to more than 120 days, and 14 were given into parental custody. Appeals from parents or relatives often released children before the completion of their terms, but it was the policy of the tribal court to keep each juvenile sentenced to jail at least a few days in his cell in order to "teach him a lesson" (Parmee 1959-1961a: 80, 82).

Various types of social pressures, derived from remnants of traditional Apache customs and beliefs, frequently caused families and individuals to become discouraged when trying to modernize or improve their home or personal conditions. More traditionally-oriented Apaches would accuse such people of being traitors to their God-given culture and becoming like "Whites." If the accused were at all sensitive to such criticisms they sometimes left the reservation or gave up their desires for modernizing (Parmee 1959-1961a: 95).

In Chapter 2 (see page 24) it has been shown how such pressures existed on many reservations, inhibiting attempts at personal achievement among students as well as adults. Both "Danny" and "Jed" had apparently felt the sting of such reprimands. Some Apaches, in fact, were convinced that these social pressures were responsible in part for the low number of Apache

---

*This charge was primarily used against juveniles who had been drinking, causing disorder, and illegally procuring liquor.

college graduates and trained Apache reservation employees (Parmee 1959-1961a: 95). Understandably, however, not all Apaches heeded these sanctions.

POLITICAL PROBLEMS

On most reservations as in many non-Indian communities, economic power and political power went hand-in-hand. The San Carlos Reservation was no exception. Agencies like the BIA and Public Health Service were permitted no part in tribal politics; but, by the mere fact of their economic potential, they acted as powerful governing forces on the reservation. The Apache tribal council, on the other hand, as was pointed out earlier in the discussion of community economic problems, was often frustrated in its efforts to legislate new programs or changes in existing ones because of its own economic impotence and its consequent dependency on alien assistance.

To the average Apache reservation inhabitant this gave not only the feeling of being dominated and of being forced into a way of life not of his own choosing, but it also had the demoralizing effect of making him feel helpless and inferior as he watched his elected leaders make often futile demands upon alien people directed by unknown or incomprehensible laws and regulations originated in a place called "Washington."*

Many Apaches today have very meager knowledge of the basic principles and designs of democratic community government. Although their traditional forms of social and political organization have long ago been changed, little has been done to teach them the fundamental tenets of the new forms of government. As a result, some Apache leaders today are not informed adequately so that they can function effectively as legislative representatives of their own local districts. This has its deleterious effects upon the people as a whole.

In 1960-61, for example, nearly every Apache interviewed was highly critical of his council. Typical comments included: The council's activities are suspect; sometimes it appears dis-

---

*For a better understanding of this phenomenon the reader is advised to study the implementation of the San Carlos and Bylas school conversion program as described in the field LOG on pages 230-309 (Parmee 1959-1961a).

interested in its own people; some leaders are self-centered; it doesn't do anything; it is often helpless in times of need (Parmee 1959-1961b: 27-29). This was more than ordinary belly-aching. It was the result of a continual lack of opportunities for the Apache people to participate in democratic government. It reflected public disfavor over the few local district meetings and the many closed council sessions; over the little effort to inform the public of the "hows" and "whys" of government operations, new programs, and changes in long-standing policies; and over much high level manipulation (Parmee 1959-1961a: 237-246, 254-256, 272-272a).

Factors Within the Family Environment

WIDESPREAD POVERTY

At the time of this study, federal, state, and private welfare programs on the San Carlos Reservation spent great sums of money to alleviate the extremely low or non-existent incomes of hundreds of Apache families.* The largest of these programs was operated by the local BIA welfare department. Not all Apaches agreed with the manner in which this program functioned, however. Criticism was chiefly aimed at the apparent lack of constructive operational goals and case records, which resulted in a rather arbitrary disbursement of funds (Parmee 1959-1961a: 154-157). There were also no apparent provisions in the program for the eventual reduction in welfare dependency among Apaches. This writer, for example, observed no efforts being made to assist families in the efficient management of their available incomes, even though it was clearly obvious that such assistance would have helped many cases.

While much of the existing poverty on the San Carlos Reservation was the result of deflated cattle incomes and higher costs of living, as well as widespread unemployment, many families became welfare cases perhaps sooner than necessary because of poor financial planning. Many incurred heavy debts through unwise buying and the over-extension of their credits

---

*Regrettably, no per-capita or total annual expenditure figures were available, but nearly all boarding school children came from welfare recipients. Elderly folks were generally on welfare.

at the local stores. The following actual case study will illustrate some of the demoralizing effects experienced by many Apache families through the excessive use of credit resources and public welfare.

The "A" family was once financially solvent. They handled most of their purchasing through one or two of the local traders who conveniently managed most of the family's financial affairs. Mrs. "A" went to the traders' stores and bought what she needed. When Mr. "A" received his cattle check twice each year he simply went to each trader and paid off his entire bill, seldom fully aware of what his money was spent for. He usually was able to cover the bill and that was all that concerned him. He felt pretty good, in fact, because at times there was some cash left over for pocket money, or perhaps for a new car or pickup. Occasionally, when Mr. "A's" bill was very high and there was not going to be much pocket money left over, he simply informed the tribal office to have his check turned over to the stores (this usually happened with a bill at some large store like the Tribal Store) and this way he did not have to bother making the transaction himself.

The "A" family managed well until the prices of cattle dropped. There was a drought and the sales had to be postponed. Then came the day when Mr. "A" could no longer pay off as many of his bills as he had before, and his credit limit was severely curtailed. This put a crimp in the "A" family's style, because they were used to much freer spending, and in fact, it took them some time to adjust to the situation. Now they had accumulated such heavy bills—in comparison to their decreased income—that the traders were forced to curtail the "A" family's credit more and more, and requested that Mr. "A's" income checks be withheld from any member of the family for fear that they would be spent before some of the bills were paid off. From this time on, Mr. "A" was lucky to even see one of his income checks, much less have the pleasure of owning it for a while. This made him very bitter.

As the years passed, Mr. "A's" family grew, and his needs increased—as did his bills—but his income from cattle did not. He worked part-time now to help out a bit, but there simply was not much work he could do on the reservation. His relationship with the traders was no longer very friendly, and he and his wife had to fight for every penny of credit they could get. Sometimes they even tried trading elsewhere, but the other traders on the reservation knew the "A" family's situation and saw that they were poor credit risks. Their requests were gracefully turned aside.

Then Mr. "A" lost his part-time job. It seemed as if Mr. "A" and his family were to face starvation. The little help they formerly received from Mrs. "A's" relatives was now turned down because they were becoming too much of a burden. There were arguments and a few fights—and that ended that. Mr. "A" cursed the stinginess of Mrs. "A's" folks and the two families refused to speak to one another. The one who felt worst of all was Mrs. "A," who was ashamed of their helplessness and sorry for the rift between their families.

Mr. "A" vented more of his anger on the traders who stoically received his abuse but offered him no further credit. Each knew he had already given in to Mr. "A" more than was good for either party. Mr. "A" even made a plea to the tribal council for a horse or a tractor so he could do some farming to help with his family's needs for food—but then he also needed seed, fertilizer, etc., etc. The council was unable to help him. Mr. "A" returned home very dejected, wondering what good the council was if it could not help him.

Mr. "A's" economic problems finally reached a climax when the new school year began. The children needed new shoes, dresses, levis, jackets, etc. and the family simply did not have the funds to cover these new items. Mr. "A" informed Mrs. "A" that she would have to pay a visit to the Welfare Office and ask at least for new clothes. Mrs. "A" was not very happy about this because she had heard that it was not easy to convince that "welfare lady" that help was needed—and besides, she was a bit ashamed to have to sit with all those other women in the waiting room, hearing their gossip about others, and knowing that they would gossip about her as soon as she had gone. Mrs. "A" had never cared to associate with them before, and now it seemed they were all in the same predicament.

It was a bit of a struggle—with the embarrassments, the language problems, and all—but Mrs. "A" finally managed to get some help from welfare. She even managed to get a couple of the older children off to boarding school. They usually kept the food bills so high and were getting a bit hard to handle, anyway, she thought. But Mrs. "A" was sorry to have to send the oldest girl away. She had become a real companion now that the family was no longer on such good terms with her relatives. Mr. "A" appeared to be getting more and more despondent, more bitter and quite complaining. He could not find a job and soon got tired of sitting around the house listening to the children make noises and Mrs. "A's" incessant chatter. He knew she was unhappy about the fight with her relatives and having to accept welfare, but there did not seem to be much he could do about it. To him, it seemed like a dirty deal all the way around: no more herd, no jobs, and the traders turning their backs whenever they saw him coming. Sometimes it all made him so mad and disgusted that he would leave his home and go off to visit with some of the other men who were hanging around like him. Some of them had the same hard-luck stories he had to tell, so at least they were sympathetic company. Once in a while if anyone had a few extra dollars, they even went over to the bootleggers and bought a few bottles of "brew." It was something to do, anyway.

The following year Mr. "A" tried to send off two more of the older children to boarding school, but he was told that the schools were all filled up. These two now had to go to public school. Mrs. "A" was really glad. She did not care to be separated from her children, even though Mr. "A" did not seem to mind it in the least. During the first week of public school it seemed as if everything was going to work out quite well, for the kids seemed to enjoy their new experience. The delight was short-lived, however, for one day one of the children brought home a bill for books and supplies. The other said he needed a special kind of gym shoes.

The children were afraid to go back to school without the money so they stayed home for the next few days while Mr. "A" went to see the chairman of the education committee and the reservation principal. He did not trust his wife in this important matter, and besides, he felt it was about time he gave those people a piece of his mind and told them what he thought of their education program. He did, too. He told them that he was a high school graduate. He was not uneducated like "some of these Indians around here." He even learned a trade. But what good did it do him? He had no job, no money. His wife had to ask for welfare. His children needed new clothes, they wanted more meat to eat—and that public school had the nerve to ask him for $12 for books and $6 for special gym shoes! What kind of a gym did they have down there, anyway, that his boy had to have special shoes to walk on it? That must be for rich people, for white people! What happened to our own high school? Everything was better then.

But Mr. "A" did not return home dissatisfied. The chairman of the education committee talked the credit manager into letting Mr. "A" have enough credit to buy the gym shoes and some more food besides, and the reservation principal called the public school and asked them to waive the costs of the books. They reluctantly complied. During the next few months when Mr. "A" received a dividend check for some special V.A. benefits, he and Mrs. "A" kept it a secret even from their friends, and then went out and spent it as they pleased. It was a long time since they had had the pleasure of such freedom. The creditors could "scratch for the money" as far as Mr. "A" was concerned. They controlled all of his cattle income by now, anyway, he lamented.

Mr. "A" and his friends complained vehemently when the tribal council tried to pass a bill for income taxes on cattle sales, but it went through. Some political machine, that council, Mr. "A" and his friends thought. There was no doubt in their minds that it was in cahoots with the trading enterprises and the public schools to exploit unfortunate Indians like themselves. They agreed such things deserved as little of their support as possible (taken from Parmee 1959-1961c: 11-17).

The ability to plan an efficient family budget is not an inherent characteristic among any people. It is a learned behavior; and many people the world over, even in countries where thrift is a matter of national pride, find it difficult to effectively assimilate this behavior. So much more difficult was it then for Apaches, who, less than four generations ago, "had been a subsistence-oriented group, operating on a seasonal basis, placing little value on thrift or on sustained labor throughout the year. . . [after which] being placed on the reservation, most of the Indians lived almost thirty years on rations provided by the United States Government" (Getty 1961-62: 185).

When, in addition, one considers the tradition of economic inter-dependence within extended family and clan relations (see pp. 25-26), as well as the apparent absence of opportunities to learn about new forms of family economics, it is of little wonder that many Apaches were inexperienced and inept in the art of budgeting. Coupled with generally low incomes and large numbers of children, such conditions caused many Apache families to be hard pressed for school clothes, books and supplies, and adequate household facilities for homework and study. It seems altogether possible that existing welfare services on the San Carlos Reservation may perpetuate the economic dependency of Apache families unless changes are made in some of its fundamental practices.

BREAKDOWN IN TRADITIONAL APACHE FAMILY RELATIONS

In Chapter 2 the significance of the traditional Apache gotah system of family authority and inter-dependency has already been discussed at some length. The present disintegration of this socio-economic institution was evidenced by the literature (Kaut 1957: 84; Marinsek 1960: 37-38) and illustrated by some of the data regarding family economics (the case of the "A" family). In addition to the obvious material effects produced by such changes, it was apparent from much of the interview data that Apache methods of child-rearing—particularly at the teen-age level—had changed considerably in form, if not in function.

It was interesting to note that while Apache parents frequently criticized teachers and school officials for reprimanding Apache children in class, many of the same parents used almost identical methods of discipline—not within the traditional setting of the gotah or household, but in the setting of the tribal court system modeled after Anglo-American patterns of jurisprudence. It was not uncommon for a parent experiencing difficulty in disciplining a teen-age child to call upon the tribal court to deal firmly with the youth, even if it meant issuing a jail term. The judge would comply; then when it was thought that the child had served long enough to have "learned a lesson," he was released into the custody of his parents (Parmee 1959-1961a: 80, 82).

The traditional element of public ridicule entered into this picture at the juvenile court hearing when parents of accused children were asked to testify against them before the entire courtroom assemblage, including judges, police officers, and other arrested youths and their parents. The following actual court incident will help to illustrate this form of behavior:

> The mother was asked to testify against her daughters. This she did with no restraint. I don't know what she said but frequently the two girls would glance at their mother with rather hurt expressions on their faces, and once in a while they would look at the floor and shake their heads negatively. Both girls were quite nervous and one was on the verge of crying, but she tried hard not to.
>
> Both were neatly dressed and sat close to one another. When the sentence was passed, the one girl nearly burst into tears, but after a few words from her sister (who seemed older) she subsided. At one time the older sister even made the younger one smile. There was obvious comradeship here and mutual support.
>
> After giving testimony, the mother simply turned her back on the two girls and walked out the door. They looked after her with blank expressions. Then, after the

hearing the girls walked away towards the prison together, arm-in-arm (Parmee 1959-1961a: 83).

Parental rejection of the two sisters was evident in the
above case, but it appeared to be off-set somewhat by sibling
"esprit de corps." In some cases, however, the parents seemed
almost vengeful by the severity of their testimonies. As one
Apache court employee put it:

> Often when the mother comes into court to testify
> against her daughter, she tries to be mean and says all
> sorts of things so her daughter won't disobey again. This
> morning, that mother told the judge all of her daughter's
> private affairs; what boyfriends she had, how she acts,
> and all kinds of things like that in order to embarrass
> the girl. That's not right. Those are private matters. Those
> are family matters which should not be discussed here
> in court in front of all these people. The daughter tries
> hard not to cry though (Parmee 1959-1961a: p. 84).

Apache court discipline was also used for drop-outs and
for children delinquent in school. In fact, during the spring
of 1959, when teen-age drop-outs had become particularly
prevalent, the tribal education committee agreed to place the
full responsibility for this problem in the hands of the tribal
judge, who promptly announced that he would put the parents
as well as the students in jail if they refused to comply with
school attendance regulations (Parmee 1959-1961a: 71-74).

Opinions regarding the constructive effectiveness of this
system of discipline varied greatly at the time. Some Apache
leaders agreed with it whole-heartedly, as the decision of the
education committee indicated. Most Anglos felt it was a cruel
and rather unconstructive way to deal with adolescents, pre-
dicting that it would have serious harmful effects on their
personalities.*

This last view appeared quite plausible, when considering
the many juvenile cases in which it was evident that current
values, behavior patterns, and institutions had failed to adequately replace their earlier traditional forms; failed for parents

---

*Opinions expressed primarily by school administrators and the
local welfare worker.

as well as children, but primarily for the children who were
expected to endure these conflicts and still return to school
each day with minds at ease, eager to assimilate the teachings
of an alien culture.

Factors Within the Program of Formal Education

SPECIAL NEEDS OF APACHES AT PRIMARY GRADE LEVELS INADEQUATELY MET BY SCHOOLS

As a starting point for the discussion of this topic, the
author again cites the words of the recent former chairman of
the San Carlos Apache Tribe:

> . . . I suspect our schools are not beginning to tackle
> adequately the basic difficulties of language—the simple
> problem of communication—of understanding and being
> understood—which confronts on all sides, the non-ac-
> culturated Indian child as he gets further along in school
> where both ideas and vocabulary become increasingly
> complex. I suspect that this failure to comprehend on
> the part of the Indian child accounts in large measure
> for the lessening of interest and enthusiasm for school,
> which I am told begins for Indian children along about
> the fifth grade (Wesley 1961: 4).

The findings of this study indeed bear out the suspicions
of Wesley quoted above. With the project office located at the
San Carlos federal day school for several months, the author
had many opportunities to observe the methods used in teaching Apache elementary students. All of the teachers at that
time, even the most dedicated ones, lacked special language
training to aid their Apache-speaking pupils. Even those teachers working with the Beginners' classes (in which nearly every
enrolled pupil knew almost no English at the start) admitted
that what they themselves lacked in training, they had to make
do with ingenuity. Teachers' meetings were seldom held and
virtually no assistance was given to the teachers during the
school year.

As the youngest Apache students moved from grade to
grade, their difficulties with language compounded as the work

became more demanding. Competition at the Indian schools was relatively light, however, since most of the teachers were taught that Indians disliked competition, although occasionally favors or prizes were won by high achievers. Low achievers were made to feel as good as the rest even though the teacher had little time to spend giving them remedial work.

Some teachers solved the problem by dividing up the classes into various ability groups for reading, arithmetic, and other subjects. In one of the classes where this author did some substitute teaching, there were no less than five such groups for reading and arithmetic. It was extremely difficult to keep four of the groups actively working while testing the recitation of the fifth group. Many were left to idle away their time after completing desk assignments. Statements made by the reservation principal at that time supported these observations.

. . . Some of this lack of interest and progress in learning is definitely the teachers' fault. Every time I walk into a class up here—and I do mean it has been the same every single time—I come in and find at least 50% of the students drawing pictures or just wasting time. And I've done this dozens of times, and it has always been the same. I think a lot of those kids are just passing the time of day (Parmee 1959-1961a: 188).

Charges and counter-charges kept shifting the blame for the slow academic progress of Apache students in the reservation day schools. Teachers blamed it on the lack of proper teaching aids and classes that were too large for the amount of remedial work needed by the students.* Another BIA educator of rank returned much of the fault to the teachers, some of whom, he said, had a "very poor" knowledge of correct English. In confirmation of his argument he recalled watching one teacher make grammatical errors in no less than eight out of ten sentences that had been written on the blackboard for students to copy (Parmee 1959-1961a: 187).

To what extent were Apache students entering the public

---

*At San Carlos Day School the classes averaged between 25 and 35 students in 1960.

schools after the fourth grade actually retarded? A Globe grammar school official stated that most entering Apache pupils were ill-prepared for public school work. Their knowledge of English was so poor that it was difficult to teach them anything new. Although remedial reading courses were offered in the Globe and Ft. Thomas schools, many Apaches apparently refused to take advantage of them (Parmee 1959-1961a: 196).

The inadequate preparation of Apache teen-age students in the higher grade levels was evident to some degree from their low grade-point averages and the extent of the age-grade lag in grades 4 through 12. One further attempt was made in 1961 to test the validity of these findings after the project staff fell heir to a considerable body of materials from one of the federal reservation school fourth grade classes; the materials consisted of the pupils' entire year's work in art, mathematics, spelling, theme-writing, English grammar, geography and science.

This material was brought for analysis and appraisal to the 1961 Workshop for Teachers of Bilingual Students, at the University of Arizona. Three public school teachers of the intermediary grade level (grades 4-6) spent several hours reviewing the work of every pupil, and came up with the following conclusions concerning both the extent of the students' scholastic progress and the nature of the teacher's techniques for instruction.

The performance of the class

a) The students with the lowest achievement test scores appeared to be "down-right illiterate," responding in a manner that was "far below the fourth grade level."

b) Those students with the highest achievement test scores produced work that might be considered to be on a par with average non-Indian public school students, but they would probably find it difficult to compete in next year's fifth grade public school class, where the competition would be greater and the work somewhat more advanced.

c) Many of the middle-ranking students of this class did work that was far below the normal fourth grade level, especially in English and mathematics. Some of their work indicated only a first grade arithmetic concept level.

d) Much of the work of the class showed "great numbers of errors, which indicated either a real lack of understanding of fundamental concepts, or carelessness from poor motivation, or both." Many of the pupils "obviously did not comprehend or try to follow the teacher's instructions on worksheets and tests."

e) According to the standard performance indicated by these materials, the evaluation committee decided that the class as a whole was "poorly prepared for fifth grade public school work."

An evaluation of the teacher's techniques

The panel of three public school teachers admitted that they were being highly critical of the teacher's techniques, by basing their judgment on the recommended standards of teaching, which are for any teacher difficult to follow precisely. They also admitted that this was not entirely an equitable appraisal because it was based primarily on the written work in class only, and not on the oral and illustrative work that presumably complemented the former in the classroom. In spite of these shortcomings, some interesting insights were revealed by the panel:

a) Judging by the written material that was presented to the class throughout the year, the teacher seemed to be "lost, groping around, and having great difficulty in coping with his pupils' academic problems."

b) His methods seemed inconsistent, unimaginative, and often confusing to the pupil; on the whole, poor planning was evident.

c) None of the tests or papers showed any corrections of the errors that were made in great numbers.

d) Some of the tests that were given to the pupils contained language errors that were made by the teacher. On the whole, the work that the teacher had prepared for his class was sloppy.

e) No apparent attempt had been made by the teacher

to insist on following instructions—or if he did, there was no noticeable improvement throughout the year.

f) Many of the work sheets that were made up for the class were so poorly worded that their instructions were unclear.

g) According to the available material, no apparent effort was made on the part of the teacher to encourage his pupils to express themselves in terms of elements from their own cultural background.

From these statements, made by experienced teachers of the fourth grade level, one could conclude that this particular class of pupils was poorly prepared to meet the demands of the integrated class in public school the following year. By the end of the year, many were not even capable of doing fourth grade work and their teacher was apparently unable to cope with the serious problem of academic retardation that faced him. The outlook for his pupils' success in the higher grade levels appeared rather dim, indeed.

DEFICIENCIES IN THE EDUCATION PROGRAM AT THE JUNIOR AND SENIOR HIGH SCHOOL LEVELS

As can be seen from the enrollment figures presented earlier in this report, the BIA San Carlos Agency was increasingly successful in its efforts to enroll Apaches in boarding school. Between 1958 and 1961, federal boarding school enrollment expanded 51.3 per cent, until it included more than 16% of the total student population on the reservation. While some agency officials (i.e., the reservation principal and the social worker) acclaimed this as an achievement, one Area Office administrator expressed concern and disapproval:

"I realize only too well that home conditions on the San Carlos Reservation are as bad as you could find anywhere, but there are altogether too many Apaches being sent to boarding school."

It was this person's opinion that the federal boarding schools were "a blessing" to many unfortunate youngsters from poor homes, but such schools were not the panacea for all the ills of Apache youngsters. It would be better, he said, to have more of them living at home, attending public school in the normal fashion with the availability of a stronger guidance program to help those who are having serious difficulties. He concluded by saying that the primary field for the solution of the educational problems at San Carlos was right on the reservation itself (Parmee 1959-1961b; 211-212).

Public school officials expressed an even dimmer view of local agency policies regarding boarding school enrollment. One administrator went so far as to say that Apaches should quit seeking "the easy way out" by going to all-Indian boarding schools, and should instead learn to "cut the mustard" in the public schools along with everyone else (Parmee, 1959-1961b: 215).

Basically, the three chief criticisms against the boarding school program were:

a) Apaches in boarding schools were isolated from non-Indians, socially as well as competitively. This isolation would eventually prolong the process of integration into Anglo society, which non-Apaches felt was a desirable thing (see above, page 7). Even some tribal officials agreed that school integration was an essential factor in the improvement of Apache education (Wesley 1961: 5).

b) None of the public school people interviewed felt that the academic standards at the boarding schools were as high as those of the average public day school. The then chairman of the tribal education committee also expressed the view that boarding school training was inadequate to meet the requirements for college preparatory training.*

c) One shortcoming in the boarding school program, criticized at various times by Apache leaders, is the lack of special facilities for the emotionally-disturbed Indian child (Wesley 1961: 6-7). Each year found teen-agers with serious personal problems being dismissed from public, mission, and even boarding schools. They returned to the reservation to generally poor home conditions and no future for which to live. Most of these students soon wound up in jail, incurring on occasion lengthy sentences, when instead they needed psy-

---

*Personal conversation with the author.

chiatric care and a more constructive environment (Parmee 1959-1961a: 24, 59-60).

At the time of this study in 1960, most Apache teen-agers were attending public schools; and, as already seen from the analysis of school records, many were in serious academic trouble. Aside from the various existing personal and home environmental factors over which the schools had no control, there were factors in the public school program itself which obstructed the successful education of Apaches. It should be stated at the outset, however, that the public schools were not entirely to blame for these deficiencies. A part of the fault lay with those who maneuvered the change-over from reser-vation Indian schools to public schools: namely, the Bureau of Indian Affairs and Apache leaders, who supported the plan without raising serious objections to its shortcomings.

Although the change-over described on pages 41-42 had begun and ended long before this study began, there was ample evidence from the interviews with school officials indicating that prior to the arrival of the first large influx of Apache students after 1949 no significant preparation had been made in the way of extra remedial facilities, curriculum adjustments, or teacher orientation (Scoggins 1959: 64). As one school administrator put it:

> We first knew about it three months before school got out. That was in the spring. In the fall of that year we had them in our schools. There wasn't any prepara-tion—other than physical and financial*—made for the change-over. It happened all at once (Parmee 1959-1961a: 199).

Considering the inadequacies in the program of the on-reservation government schools, it is not difficult to understand the extreme handicaps many Apaches must have felt in the public school education program without any of the provisions mentioned above. Even by 1960, nearly ten years after the first large group of Apaches had entered the public high schools, little had been achieved in the way of devising special aca-

---

*Referring to enlargement of the physical plant and staff, and establishment of Johnson-O'Malley support.

demic programs for the Indian students beyond the limited acceleration of remedial reading facilities (Parmee 1959-1961a: 196).

Instead of tribal, BIA, and public school cooperation in a planned program that might have aided Apache youngsters with the transition from federal to public schools, the public schools were apparently left on their own to make the best of it. Some did by putting Apaches in so-called "slow-groups" (Parmee 1959-1961a: 197-198), and by granting social promotions to a large number. At Globe the guidance counselor was expected to allot half his working time to Indian student problems, while at Ft. Thomas the school superintendent-principal made himself available at all times for such purposes.*

In spite of the available counseling services in the public schools, the standard methods for evaluating the nature and extent of Apache personal and academic problems and the techniques for measuring individual Apache potentials and interests seemed quite inadequate. Bernardoni's findings, described on pages 56-59, at least showed the shortcomings and pitfalls inherent in tests like the Lorge-Thorndike series, when using them to compare Indians with non-Indians (Bernardoni 1960: 11). Where language differences made comprehension of the test difficult for the student and the lack of a double set of known cultural standards obstructed the testor's comparison of the responses, such devices could only be partially successful in achieving the goals for which they were intended.

It was also evident at the time of this study that some of the schools, and especially the BIA agency, were not maintaining adequate records for the purpose of periodically evaluating the students' progress and the program's effectiveness. All of the data summaries presented thus far, with the exception of the school enrollment figures and the Lorge-Thorndike

*The guidance counselor at Globe was reputed to have spent very little time doing any counseling at all (Parmee 1959-1961a: 196-197). In fact, he himself admitted to the author once that very few Indian students (boys in particular) ever came to him with problems [notes from case history of "Bert"]. This perhaps explains in part why some Apache students like "Bert" did not even know of the counselor's services.

test results, were collected and organized by the project staff. Although each student had his individual record file at the school he was currently attending, the author knew of no efforts on the part of school administrators to compile such records into periodic summaries for the purposes of trend evaluations* (Parmee 1959-1961b: 1-6).

At times it appeared that school staff evaluations of Apaches expressed more of personal views and impressions than validated findings. A brief sample of collected comments should suffice to illustrate this point:

> They [Apaches] could work as well as other students if they would get out of their I-don't-care attitudes (public school teachers) (Parmee 1959-1961a: 193).
>
> Apaches are one of the smartest Indian tribes in the Southwest, and also one of the most hostile, most stubborn, and meanest. . . . They are a bit lazy, too (public school employee) Parmee 1959-1961a: 213-214).
>
> The trouble is, these [Apache] people don't want education. They think it's poison. They hold ceremonies every year to do away with all the evils their kids have picked up in school! (reservation school principal) (Crumrine 1959: 29).
>
> Apaches are at the bottom of the barrel as far as Indians go. They are the dumbest and worst off economically. They don't want to be educated, and they don't want to get out from under the government (public school counselor) (Crumrine 1959: 40).

It would have been difficult to estimate how many non-Apache school personnel shared these views, but it was plain enough to see that prejudice was not restricted to any one school or occupational level. Some of these views among public school people remained because few ever came on the reservation to see things for themselves. Out of the few who did, some went back with their suspicions even more strongly confirmed than before—or so they said.

---

*The record of one year's total absences by the Bylas school principal was the sole exception known.

CONFLICTS ARISING OUT OF THE ORIENTATION OF THE EDUCATION PROGRAM

Thus far, much has been said about the lack of Apache participation in the operation of the education program. This alien management of a key reservation development program did not permit Apaches to guide the fate of their own future, nor did it provide them with the opportunities for learning how to do so (Wesley 1961: 7). Apaches resented being denied this privilege and did what they could to fight against it (Parmee 1959-1961a: 230-309).

A second fundamental criticism that Apache leaders expressed again and again in opposition to the education program evolved out of a conflict of basic goals for the program.

I realize the fact that there are people who talk about integration, assimilation, acculturation, first class citizenship, etc. But you know the American Indians have something different that was bestowed upon them by the grace of God, such as our songs, tribal dances, arts and crafts, our religion, games and stories. Some of these are fast disappearing and my question is: are we going to continue to lose these precious gifts through this process of education or becoming White men? Or should we continue to identify ourselves as Indians, which to me is no disgrace. (Wesley 1961: 7).

The "people" Wesley referred to were the administrators of agencies managing Indian affairs, school officials, and off-reservation politicians. It was these people, who by means of their economic and political power and their educational advantage held the fate of many reservation programs in their hands. Directing programs of integration to facilitate the earliest possible assimilation of Indians into the larger American culture was a primary orientation of their thoughts and actions.

This orientation was expressed in their public speeches (Head 1960: 24), in their programs of relocation, public school integration (Parmee 1959-1961a: 197, 301), and tribal government, and in their day-to-day dealings with Indians (Parmee 1959-1961a: 301). Tribal leaders like Annie Wauneka (1963) and Clarence Wesley (1961) tended to react negatively to this imposed Anglo orientation of Indian programs, as did many of their followers, even though they worked hard to bring such programs to their respective reservations. Thus, while they feared that the implementation of these programs might on the one hand accelerate the extinction of Indian culture, they also could not deny the fact that formal education was a key factor in solving existing social and economic problems, by raising the educational standards of their people.

Apache teen-agers did not express the same fears as the older generation. From the many student interviews and case histories, like those presented in this study, it was evident that some were not so concerned about the future—not even their own, much less the future of their whole tribe. On the other hand, others, such as "Jed," felt they could be educated and still remain Apache. To them "Apache" had a different meaning from that of the "old folks." It was less characterized perhaps by ancient ceremonials, mythology, and socio-religious customs, but it meant "Apache" nevertheless, and its principal features were clearly modern. As the new-generation Apache tribal chairman described it:

> If we have better housing, health, better jobs on the reservation, does this mean that we won't be Indians anymore? No, it doesn't. If an Indian wants to be an Indian he can be one all of his life. You don't forget your Indian upbringing easily, even when you have the highest education (Mull 1963: 30-31).

Older, more tradition-oriented Apaches like Wesley failed to see things quite this way. Much of their lives' efforts were spent in trying to preserve the many unique traditional aspects of Apache culture that were "bestowed upon them by the grace of God" (Wesley 1961: 7). Less educated Apaches, however, could not always, like Wesley, see the positive as well as the negative effects of education, and their resistance to many programs of modernization directly influenced the lives of their children, for it made understanding difficult between the young and the old, and added further to the already staggering proportions of existing teen-age problems.

CHAPTER 5

Relevant Issues and Observations

THE PROGRAM OF EDUCATION for San Carlos Apaches, represented in the main by federal and public education agencies during 1959-1961, failed to achieve its stated objectives of educating and integrating Apache children for the mainstream of American life because it was not a community-wide program of academic and fundamental education, designed to meet the specific local needs of *all* age groups in the Apache society. As such, it ignored the importance of the relationship between each child and the family-community environment in which he was raised.

The existing program sought to teach only the younger generations of Apaches in the hope that they would eventually acquire the same values, literacy, and job-skills as the non-Indians. Lacking in adequate counseling and remedial services for most handicapped Apache students, however, the program was unable to overcome some of the most basic academic problems.

Meanwhile, those responsible for the program impeded the efforts of the schools even further by neglecting to give Apache parents and leaders the opportunity to raise their own educational standards. This would have required a special program of fundamental education and encouragement of more active participation in community affairs. This sort of preparation would have enabled many adults to function more effectively in support of their children and the program as a whole, a role which they were expected to fulfill.

At a now famous conference of educators and anthropologists, Bernard Siegel (1955: 38-49) discussed the basic channels through which "explicit culture" reaches the child in the modern American community.

Channel I: Educational Institutions

1) In the academic community the form and meaning of transmitted material enter this channel through the teachers of teachers.

2) The teachers and administrators of the community schools determine what enters the school system itself in accordance with their own values and motivations.

Channel II: Peer Groups and Cliques

1) Here the most constant and consistent kinds of action patterns and attitudes are instilled, providing influences that will often override school and family teachings.

2) Participation in peer groups and cliques is often an index of unsatisfied needs or frustations felt within the school system.

Channel III: The Home

1) The hierarchy of values, beliefs, and behavior patterns of parents are usually reinforced by kinsmen and family friends.

At San Carlos, it seemed that the last two channels— peer groups and home influences—were not regarded by local educators as potentially constructive sources of Apache education; hence, there was no attempt to adapt and include them as a part of the formal educative process. On the contrary, efforts were made to remove young Apaches from their home and peer-group environments by sending as many as possible to the federal and mission boarding schools. Except, perhaps, for a few extreme "skid-row" cases, this attempt to divorce students from distinctive Apache ways developed in the reservation milieu did not succeed. As long as there existed an Apache reservation, there lived an Apache people with a distinct Apache language and heritage and a way of life that could be attributed solely to them. To the overwhelming majority of Indians born and raised in this place, it was "home" in every known sense of the word. In spite of the poverty, social ills, and political conflicts that prevailed there, it was nevertheless the only spot on the globe that belonged undisputedly to the Apaches, and it symbolized for many their past, present, and promise of a future.

By refusing to accept family and community influences as a part of the education of Apache teen-agers, the program initiated by the Whites became a major source of confusion and frustration, rather than one of motivation and learning. At home on the reservation, many children were taught to respect traditional beliefs and taboos, to learn their native tongue, and to behave in the manner of their elders. In school, these same children were being compelled to learn English and were scolded for speaking Apache. They were being exposed to books that depicted their ancestors as thieves and murderers, while the White man was shown as the highest achievement of civilization. In school, these same teen-agers were told that the environment of their home—their reservation— was corruptive and degrading, and opposed to progress. Such was the prevailing atmosphere of learning.

From the very start of his schooling, the average Apache child suffered handicaps: the deprivations of his home life (i.e., poverty, drinking, illiteracy, socio-cultural disintegration) and the incompatibilities of his unique heritage with the dominant Anglo culture (i.e., language, values, beliefs). The schools were for the most part unprepared to assist the Apache child in overcoming these handicaps. Adequate remedial training was lacking, counseling services were weak and ineffective in handling the often unique Apache problems, and much of the orientation of the program was at odds with the goals and needs expressed by the Apache people.

In most cases, as the student moved on from grade to grade, finally entering into the integrated public school system, the academic, social, and financial demands sharply increased. Apaches had to compete with Anglos, who were more intellectually motivated and socially aggressive, and whose ethnic background more directly coincided with the school curriculum and disciplinary methods. Off the reservation in a less secure environment of limited social acceptance, particularly within the peer-group structure, Apaches were faced with the additional problem of adjusting to the question of their social identity and of accepting the values and behavior patterns established within each status ascribed.

Many of the Apache students interviewed at the time of this study soon realized, after entering the off-reservation public schools, that the patterns had long since been established. Their cultural differences were now more pronounced than ever in the mixed ethnic environment. Not only were appearances, interests, and overt mannerisms different, language discrepancies made even casual communication with Anglos somewhat difficult. Consequently, Apache children sought and quickly found security within their own Apache cliques.

In the classrooms Anglo-Apache differences reached their extremes. As the complexity of the curriculum mounted from grade level to grade level, the intensity of the problems worsened for the Apaches. Some were shuffled into retarded classes, while others were merely passed along with social promotions. Although no one—Anglo or Apache—ever openly admitted it, it was difficult to hide the fact that the Apaches comprised the major portion of the school problem cases.

While educators, tribal leaders and elders urged Apache teen-agers to meet the growing challenges of the future through higher education, for many the task became increasingly futile. In the midst of these frustrations, some students simply withdrew into themselves and retired from the scene, first mentally, then physically. Then they were marked as drop-outs. Others sought support from the limited sources available to them: the peer group, the family or elders, and outside agencies or acquaintances.

The Apache teen-age peer group could offer very little in the way of constructive support for school problems, for it consisted primarily of other frustrated students experiencing basically the same problems. They could offer sympathy and comradeship through clique or gang activities (i.e., walking around at night, drinking, mischief-making at ceremonials, etc.), and by expounding the rejection of academic goals as being "White" and not "Apache." Those students not willing to accept these negative values and the related philosophy of despair risked being branded as "White" and losing many peer friends. A rare few, like "Danny" and "Jed," mustered the courage to break away from their peers, but they had by then found outside sources of support to rely on.

A chief source of support for the Apache teen-ager might have been the family or elders, but in a great number of cases this potential source had not been prepared for the responsibilities that now were imposed upon it by the modern educational system. The educators, who so ardently implored the support of Apache parents and in fact depended heavily upon them, had made no provisions to teach parents how to comply with their responsibilities. The school system had even ignored their requests for assistance and their desire to share in the task of running the program.

Neglecting to give Apache parents and tribal leaders an active role in the design and operation of their community education system not only gave rise to a bitter resentment among much of the adult population (which was then passed on to many students), but it also left many cooperative parents and elders helpless in sharing the burdens of their children. As the traditional extended family system of mutual support deteriorated, more and more of the burden of raising children fell upon the shoulders of the parents. But as the children proceeded up the academic ladder, there grew a kind of progressive alienation between the two generations that made parental assistance increasingly unattainable. This alienation was primarily the result of the vast discrepancy in educational and experiential backgrounds between the students and adults, and it succeeded in compounding the frustrations of both groups as they struggled with the problems of their swiftly changing environment.

Considering, then, the spread and severity of personal, family, and community problems among the San Carlos Apaches, it is not difficult to understand why so many teen-agers were failing in school, taking to drink, and feeling despondent and apathetic about their future career possibilities. Unable to help each other, Apache students and parents were frequently dependent upon outside sources for assistance. While this procedure did at times avert a family crisis, the sources were in the author's opinion far too inadequate to cope with the majority of day-to-day minor crises that occurred, which frequently grew into insoluble dilemmas. While teachers often expressed a certain degree of sympathy for their Apache students, they generally had little contact or experience with reservation life, and they were at a loss as to how to assist.

As mentioned earlier, the extent of counseling services for both Apache students and parents was quite meager in 1960, and the few individuals involved could not begin to attack the root causes of the problems discussed above. Neither could the principal, the school counselor, nor the tribal juvenile officer begin to bridge the gap left by years of neglect in such areas as adult education and local community management.

At the conclusion of the study it was evident that certain actions seemed warranted in order to bring about significant improvement in the education of San Carlos Apaches. Such actions might include:

1) an intensive community-wide training program to improve adult educational standards and increase adult understanding of community problems and programs in order to qualify more Apaches for participation in local education and development projects;

2) On-the-job training programs and special courses for all Apache political leaders and officials to assist them in improving the performance of their assigned duties, and to help them comprehend more fully the fundamentals of modern community government;

3) improved and increased relationships between the schools and Apache families and community groups to expand their share of participation in the program and to increase the knowledge of school teachers and administrators about Apache culture, motivations, and problems;

4) improved and expanded guidance and rehabilitation services for students and their families with programs involving drinking, marital conflicts, child-rearing, school work, etc., as well as the exploration of better methods for measuring Apache student potentials and defining problems.

5) increased remedial training for Apaches in school with

serious language handicaps and retardation in other academic subject areas; the use of remedial summer school sessions with Apache adults as volunteer instructors; procedure allowing Apache "Beginners" to enroll in regular school sessions at the age of five years;

6) a selection of courses on Apache culture and history in the curriculum of education for Apache youngsters in order to acquaint them with their past heritage and to dispel existing distortions of fact resulting from years of prejudice;

7) expanded student summer employment, exploring the possibilities of apprenticeship programs in job skills applicable to reservation employment needs;

8) and finally, the establishment of a new policy prevailing over all others throughout the direction and operation of the program of education for Apaches: *The only manner of achieving a successful program is by seeing to it that it is designed to meet specific needs, to include active Apache participation in every phase, and to have as its ultimate goal, a stronger, healthier, and more self-sustaining Apache reservation community with a progressive citizenry.*

As anthropologist Margaret Mead once wrote:

If the new education is to fill the place of the old, it has to cover all areas of living. Native education included growing-up; it gave instruction in inter-personal relationships, soil conservation, and ways of making a living. The task of fundamental education is to cover the whole of living. In addition, it is to teach not only new ways, but the need and incentive for new ways (Mead, et al. 1955: 253).

With the new conception of education as covering all areas of living came the recognition of society as the unit to be educated (Mead, et al. 1955: 254).

Education is needed in all these areas to cope with and repair the destruction already introduced; and beyond this, to make it possible for the people if they choose, to take their place in the community of nations, and to take advantage of the progress of science and technology in improving their standard of living (Mead, et al. 1955: 253).

A Review of Developments Since 1961

In 1966, the author toured the San Carlos Reservation and adjacent areas to interview local education officials. From their comments it was evident that some significant changes had occurred in certain phases of the program of education for Apaches.

Shortly after the conclusion of the project, the Bylas federal day school was closed down and all the Bylas school-aged children (except for those in boarding and mission schools) were bussed into the newly-expanded public school facilities at Ft. Thomas. In an effort to cope with some of the special needs of this increased Apache enrollment—Apache students now comprise between 75% and 80% of the total student body—Ft. Thomas educators introduced new methods of testing and evaluation. Out of this evolved a program of non-graded classes for students between grade levels 1 through 8. A much stronger emphasis was placed upon reading throughout the Ft. Thomas program, and new facilities in the form of a reading lab and a resource center were added. Specialized training for teachers through a project sponsored by the Kellogg Foundation with the University of Arizona also helped the staff at Ft. Thomas to strengthen their approach to the solution of educational problems.

Globe Public Schools, meanwhile, made an attempt to improve their guidance program with the establishment of a full-time Indian counselor.

At San Carlos the Bureau of Indian Affairs is gradually phasing out its day school program, converting the facilities into a local public school system called Rice School District. Apache children are now permitted to enter kindergarten at the age of 5 years, and steps are being taken to reduce the size of classes to 25 students. Regular staff meetings and special orientation projects for San Carlos teachers are also helping to improve teacher preparedness for coping with Apache student problems. A remedial reading program has also been started at San Carlos, and with the help of Public Law 89-10 under the Elementary and Secondary Education Act of 1965, adult education classes have begun. Thus far

(May, 1966), the curriculum appears to be limited to primarily academic subjects, such as English, mathematics, reading, etc. and the enrollment is quite small.

After the appointment of an Apache Community Action Program Director in early 1966, the number of Apaches involved in community development work on the reservation has increased considerably. A PTA has also been under way at San Carlos during the last two years, with approximately 90 paid members, mostly Apaches (according to a statement by the Reservation Principal). An Apache housewife was elected chairman in 1966. In both Ft. Thomas and Rice Public School districts, Apaches have been elected to serve on the local school boards, a milestone in the history of Apache education.

In spite of the new developments described above, it was apparent from the interviews with school officials that many of the fundamental problems in Apache education still exist. Surveys by school officials revealed the majority of Apache students in the intermediate grade levels (5, 6, and 7) to be two to four years below the normal reading standards for their grades. Social promotions are still prevalent as are drop-outs and transfers. In one school, teachers identified 160 out of approximately 450 enrolled Apaches as exceedingly unresponsive to the teachers' efforts in class. The categories of suggested problems under which these students were listed included: withdrawn, may need psychiatric help, retardation, may need specialized education. Inadequate academic preparation in the primary grades was still cited as a major cause of academic problems at the higher grade levels.

Social and economic problems affecting the education of Apache youngsters, and stemming primarily from inadequacies within the family and community environment, apparently continue to justify a proportionately high enrollment of Apaches in the boarding schools. In 1966, at least 25% out of a total tribal enrollment of 1,800 pupils was sent away to boarding school, according to a local BIA official. Poverty, drinking, and broken homes were given as some of the primary problems for these Apache children. Another school official said he was discouraged by the increasing number of Apache high school graduates who have taken to drink and idleness, when their performance in school predicted a much brighter future.

Within the reservation community, poverty and unemployment remain at a very high rate. The lack of funds was cited as a major factor contributing to the decline in activities of the Tribal Education Committee. Although federal Poverty Program funds have been applied to the local economy in different ways, sudden program changes have already made some Apaches wary of the reliability of these funds as a consistent means of support. There apparently is also some feeling among officials and local Apaches that Bylas does not experience its due share of involvement in some of these new development programs.

It is certainly not for this author to say, without the benefit of further investigation, what favorable effects the recent developments in Apache education will have in the long run. While some improvements are evident, particularly within the public school programs and the sole remaining BIA reservation day school, one cannot help but wonder if this is just a hand against the tide of vastly greater and more complex social and economic problems which have inundated virtually every aspect of present day reservation life for Apaches. It is this life which is in conflict with the environment of the schools. Its chaotic nature undermines each day the work of the carefully planned, systematized, and progressive program of formal education for Apache children, and it is the children themselves who must suffer the consequences along with their parents, who sit helplessly by the wayside and watch. This helplessness and the prolonged frustration that comes from years of having to accept one's fate from the hands of others can demoralize even the proudest of people as it has many Apaches.

There seems to be a greater awareness today on the San Carlos Reservation of the need to involve more Apaches in community affairs. This is a hopeful sign, and some of the federal Poverty Programs have helped to clear the path enabling Apaches to take hold of new responsibilities. But what if the funds supporting these programs should fail a few short years from now? In the light of present economic conditions on the reservation, the answer seems all too obvious.

Until the San Carlos Apaches are able to secure a stable economy on the reservation which can provide a more adequate source of income and employment for the people, they will remain at the mercy of outside resources which can be here today and gone tomorrow, depending upon the whims of a great many complex social, political, and economic factors that are far beyond the reach of local Apache influences. And unless these outside resources, regardless of their immediate objectives, include the education and progressive involvement of Apaches in all facets of community life, their benefits to the people will be short-lived and of questionable value.

Selected Bibliography

Arizona Commission of Indian Affairs
   1961-1962   *Federal and State Participation In Indian Education.*
                Phoenix.
   1964a   *Reservation Survey: Education.* Phoenix.
   1964b   *Survey of the San Carlos Reservation.* Phoenix (confidential).

Artichoker, J. Jr. and N. M. Palmer
   1959   *The Sioux Indian Goes to College.* Institute of Indian Studies, State University of South Dakota, Vermillion, South Dakota.

Barnett, H. G.
   1953   *Innovation: The Basis for Cultural Change.* McGraw-Hill Book Co., Inc., New York.

Beatty, W. W.
   1953   *Education for Cultural Change.* Bureau of Indian Affairs, Chilocco, Oklahoma.

Bennett, R. and L. Coombs
   1964   Effective Education to Meet Special Needs of Native Children. *Journal of American Indian Education.* Vol. 3, No. 3: 21-25. Tempe, Arizona.

Bernardoni, L. C.
   1960   Analysis of Results of Lorge-Thorndike Intelligence Tests with Apache Students. Personal communication.
   1962   Apache Parents and Vocational Choice. *Journal of American Indian Education* Vol. 2, No. 2: 1-8. Tempe, Arizona.

Boyce, G.
   1960   Why Do Indians Quit School? *Indian Education* 344: 4-8. Washington, D.C.

Boyd, W.
   1952   *The History of Western Education.* Adam and Charles Black, London.

Bureau of Indian Affairs
   1956   62 Indian Affairs Manual. Mimeographed. Washington, D. C. March 2, 1956.

119

Commission on the Rights, Liberties, and Responsibilities of the American Indian
1961   A Program for Indian Citizens. The Fund for the Republic, Albuquerque.

Condie, L.
1958   The Effect of Cultural Difference in the Education of Navajo Indians. University of New Mexico. Albuquerque.

Crumrine, L. S.
1959   Field Notes from San Carlos. MS. Arizona-Sonora Files. University of Arizona, Tucson.

Dozier, E. P., G. E. Simpson, and J. M. Yinger
1957   The Integration of Americans of Indian Descent. The Annals of the American Academy of Political and Social Science. Vol. 311: 158-165. Philadelphia.

Fey, H. E. and D. McNickle
1959   Indians and Other Americans. Hayer and Brothers, New York.

Getty, H. T.
1961-1962   San Carlos Apache Cattle Industry. Human Organization. Vol. 20, No. 4: 181-186. Ithica.

Gonzales, R.
1963   A Comparison of Indian and Non-Indian Achievement in the Parker Schools. Annual Conference of the Coordinating Council for Research in Indian Education. Phoenix: 56-70.

Goodwin, G.
1942   The Social Organization of the Western Apache. University of Chicago Press, Chicago.

Green, E.
1962   Six Families View Education from the Hogan. Annual Conference of the Coordinating Council for Research in Indian Education. Phoenix: 116-124.

Greenberg, N. C.
1964   Administrative Problems Related to Integration of Navajo Indians in Public Education. Doctoral Dissertation. University Microfilms, Inc., Ann Arbor.

Havighurst, R. J. and B. L. Neugarten
1955   American Indian and White Children. University of Chicago Press, Chicago.

Havighurst, R. J.
1957   Education Among American Indians: Individual and Cultural Aspects. The Annals of the American Academy of Political and Social Science. Vol. 311: 105-115. Philadelphia.

Head, W.
1960   The Navajo People and the Future. Third Annual Conference on Navajo Education. Flagstaff, Arizona: 23-24.

Jacobsen, J. V.
1938   Educational Foundations of the Jesuits in Sixteenth Century New Spain. University of California Press, Berkeley.

Kardiner, A.
1939   The Individual and His Society. Columbia University Press, New York.

Kaut, C.
1957   *The Western Apache Clan System.* University of New Mexico Publications in Anthropology. No. 9. Albuquerque.

Keay, F. E.
1959   *A History of Education in India and Pakistan.* Oxford University Press, Calcutta.

Keesing, F.
1958   *Cultural Anthropology: The Science of Custom.* Rinehart and Company, Inc., New York.

King, W.
1954   *Cross Cultural Factors in Health Administration. Indian Health in Arizona.* University of Arizona Press, Bertram K. Kraus, ed., Tucson.

Linton, R.
1936   *The Study of Man.* Appleton-Century-Crofts, Inc., New York.

Macgregor, G.
1946   *Warriors Without Weapons.* University of Chicago Press, Chicago.

Marinsek, E. A.
1960   *The Effect of Cultural Difference in the Education of Apache Indians.* University of New Mexico, Albuquerque.

McCombe, L., E. Z. Vogt, and C. Kluckhohn
1951   *Navajo Means People.* Harvard University Press, Cambridge.

McCully, B. T.
1940   *English Education and the Origins of Indian Nationalism.* Columbia University Press, New York.

McGrath, G. D.
1962   *Higher Education of Southwestern Indians With Reference to Success and Failure.* Arizona State University Cooperative Research Project No. 938, Tempe, Arizona.

Mead, M.
1955   *Cultural Patterns and Technical Change.* New American Library, New York.

Mull, M.
1963   Mimeographed speech. *Fourth Annual Indian Education Conference.* Arizona State University, Tempe, Arizona: 30-33.

Officer, J.
1956   *Indians In School.* Bureau of Ethnic Research, University of Arizona, Tucson.

Oliger, M.
1961   The Impact of Transition from Bureau to Public School. *Annual Conference of the Coordinating Council for Research in Indian Education.* Phoenix: 8-10.

Opler, M. O.
1946   *Childhood and Youth in Jicarilla Apache Society.* Hodge Publication Fund. Vol. V, Los Angeles.

Orata, P.
1953   *Fundamental Education in an Amerindian Community.* Haskell Institute, Bureau of Indian Affairs, Lawrence, Kansas.

122   *Bibliography*

Parmee, E. A.
1959-1961   a. San Carlos Field Log. MS. Arizona-Sonora Files,
                University of Arizona, Tucson.
                b. San Carlos Report. MS. Arizona-Sonora Files,
                University of Arizona, Tucson.
                c. Basic Outline of San Carlos Report: Topic III.
                MS. Arizona-Sonora Files, University of Arizona,
                Tucson.
1961   Social Factors Affecting the Education of San Carlos
                Apaches. *Annual Conference of the Coordinating
                Council for Research in Indian Education.* Phoenix:
                22-26.
Peterson, S.
1948   *How Well Are Indian Children Educated?* United
                States Indian Service, Lawrence, Kansas.
Phoenix Indian School
1960   A Summary of the Workshop on the Emotional
                Needs and Problems of Indian Students in Boarding
                Schools. Mimeographed. Phoenix.
Prucha, F. P.
1962   *American Indian Policy in the Formative Years.*
                Harvard University Press, Cambridge.
Radcliffe-Brown, A. R.
1952   *Structure and Function in Primitive Society.* The
                Free Press, Glencoe, Illinois.
Redfield, R.
1960   *The Little Community and Peasant Society and Cul-
                ture.* University of Chicago Press, Chicago.
Riesman, D., N. Glazer, and R. Denney
1955   Character and Society. *Studies in Motivation.* D. C.
                McClelland, ed. Appleton-Century-Crofts, Inc., New
                York: 252-265.
Robison, H. E., E. H. Spicer, et al.
1954   *The San Carlos Apache Indian Reservation: A Re-
                sources Development Study.* Stanford Research In-
                stitute, Phoenix.
Sanchez, G. I.
1944   *The Development of Higher Education in Mexico.*
                Kings Crown Press, New York.
Siegel, B. J.
1955   Models for the Analysis of the Educative Process
                in American Communities. *Education and Anthro-
                pology.* George D. Spindler, ed. Stanford Univer-
                sity Press: Stanford: 38-49.
Spicer, E. H.
1962   *Cycles of Conquest.* University of Arizona Press,
                Tucson.
Spindler, G. D.
1963   *Education and Culture.* Holt, Rinehart and Winston,
                Inc., New York.
Thompson, H.
1960   Research and Its Implications for Indian Educa-
                tion: From the Launching Pad to the Moon. *Third
                Annual Conference on Navajo Education.* Flagstaff,
                Arizona: 12-15.

Wauneka, A.
1963   Recorded speech. *Fourth Annual Indian Education
              Conference.* Arizona State University, Tempe, Ari-
              zona: 33-37.
Wax, M.
1963   American Indian Education as a Cultural Trans-
              action. *Teachers College Record.* Vol. 64, No. 8:
              693-704, New York.
Wax, M. and R. Wax
1963   The Oglala Sioux Educational Project. Mimeo-
              graphed, confidential. Emory University, Atlanta.
1964   Cultural Deprivation as an Educational Ideology.
              Journal of American Indian Education. Vol. 3, No.
              2: 15-18. Tempe, Arizona.
Wesley, C.
1961   Indian Education. *Journal of American Indian Edu-
              cation.* Vol. 1, No. 1: 4-7. Tempe, Arizona.
Zintz, M. V.
1960   *The Indian Research Study: Final Report.* Univer-
              sity of New Mexico, Albuquerque.

Index

Apache students (cont.)

socialization, 25, *See also* Family; Parents, Traditonal culture

summer employment, 48, 114

vocational choices, 23, 24, 68

See also Academic achievement in school; Boarding schools; Day schools; Education program; Illness; Public schools

Application of the data, viii, ix, 9

Arizona State Department of Public Instruction, 56

Arizona Commission of Indian Affairs, 15, 19, 31, 68, 81, 82

Attendance in school, 43-55

"attendance scale," 43-44

causes of absenteeism, 47-55

extent of attendance problem, 43-47, 49

See also Case studies

Beatty, W.W., 27

Beginners, Apache attitudes towards, 39

minimum age, 34, 62, 114

problems of, 97

Bennett, R.L., and Coombs, L.M., 30, 31

Bernardoni, L.C., 23, 24, 56-59, 104

Bishops' schools, 11

Boarding schools, administration, 35, 43

Apache attitudes towards, 41-42

Apache enrollment in, 34, 39-41, 101, 116

Apache grade levels, 62-64

chief criticisms of, 101-103

consequences of Indian Reorganization Act., 14, 15

curriculum, 35

establishment of, 14

influence on attendance and enrollment records, 45, 64

lack of non-Indian competition, 61, 102

Phoenix Indian School, 34, 62-64

selection for enrollment in, 35, 48, 116

Sherman Institute, 34

Stewart Indian School, 34

student problems in, 18, 19, 48, 61

Theodore Roosevelt Boarding School, 34

under auspices of Christian missions, 14

See also Teachers

Boyce, G., 46

Boyd, W., 10, 11

British colonial policies, in India, 11-12

in tribal America, 12-13

Bureau of Indian Affairs, criteria for the selection of boarding school students, 35

education, 4, 14, 30-31, 41, *See also* Indian education

hostilities and prejudices towards Indians, 29

"ideology of cultural deprivation," 29

schools, 4, 14, 34, 35, 39-42, *See also* Day schools; Boarding schools

termination of services, 28

See also Education program; San Carlos Indian Agency (BIA)

Bylas, 2, 3, 44

problems unique to, 44, 117

See also Day schools

Case studies, 21-23, 53-54, 70-81, 90-94

Cattle raising, *see* San Carlos Apaches

Christianity, influences of on culture change process, 1, 2

Christian missions, Apache student enrollment in, 34, 39-42

church influence on early education, 10, 11